GIRLS' LAST TOUR

2

TSUKUMIZU

GIRLS' LAST TOUR

09

09 PHOTOGRAPHS

READY?

THREE. TWO. ONE.

SAY, "CHEESE."

KASHA (SNAP)

(WHRR)

WHAT'S "CHEESE"?
BEATS ME.
カチ
KACHI (CLICK)
I SAW THEM DO THAT BEFORE TAKING A PICTURE IN A BOOK ONCE.
カチ
KACHI
HMMM...

IS IT JUST ME, OR IS IT REALLY WHITE?
MAYBE THE EXPOSURE WAS SET TOO HIGH...
MAYBE YOU'RE A LOUSY SHOT.
WHAT WAS THAT?

OKAY, LET'S GET GOING.
THE MORE GROUND WE COVER BEFORE DARK, THE BETTER.

HUP!
GI (CREAK)

TOTOTOTO (PUTTER)

SFX: TOTOTOTOTOTOTO (PUTTER)

LET ME SEE IT.
DON'T BREAK IT.

YOU WORRY TOO MUCH.
KASHI (CLACK)
KACHI (CLICK)

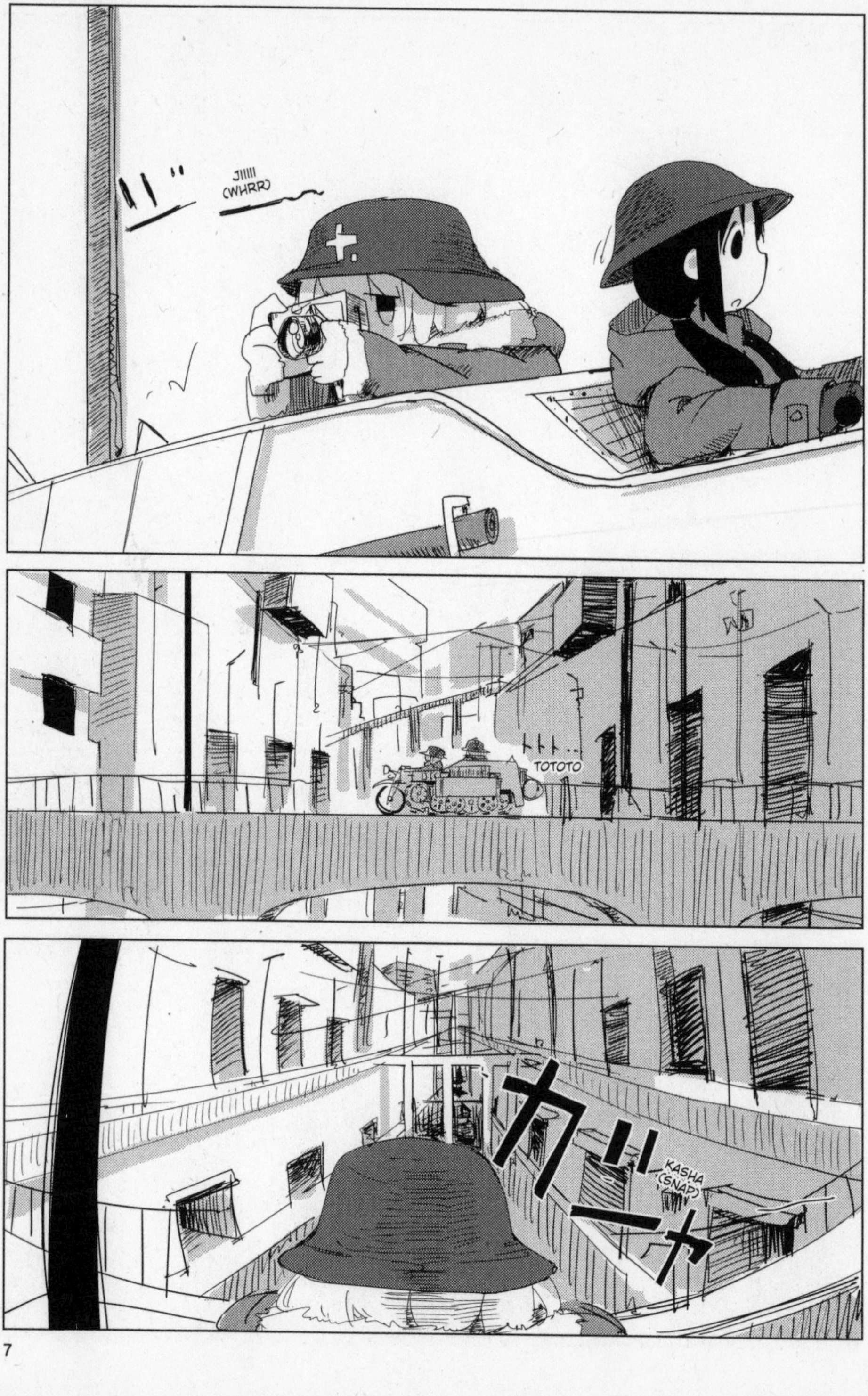

JIIIII
(WHRR)

TOTOTO

カシャ
KASHA
(SNAP)

WELL?
SFX: TOTOTOTOTOTOTO (PUTTER)

IT'S BLURRY.

YOU CAN USE THE DIAL ON THE FRONT TO ADJUST THE FOCUS.

(WHRR)
THIS THING?

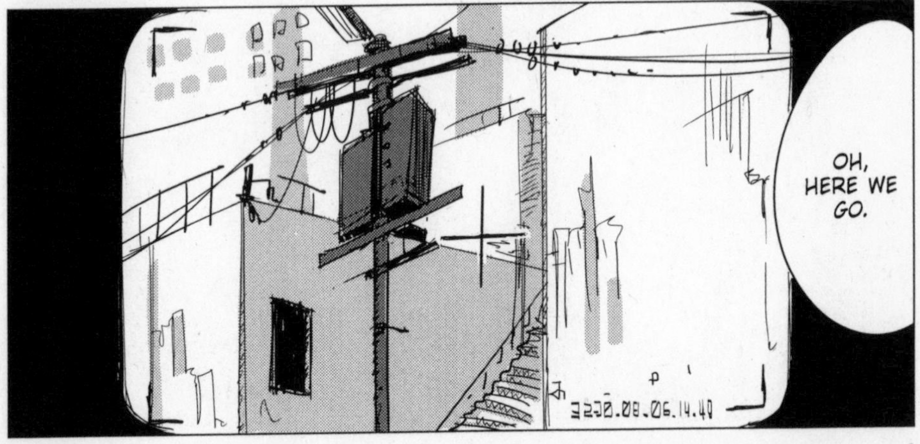
OH, HERE WE GO.
3230.08.06.14.40

IF KANAZAWA WAS GOING TO GIVE THIS TO US...
TOTOTOTOTO
...HE SHOULD HAVE AT LEAST TAUGHT US HOW TO USE IT.

OH! BEFORE WE GO OUR SEPARATE WAYS...
...I WANT TO GIVE YOU THIS AS THANKS FOR SHARING YOUR FOOD WITH ME.
WHAT IS IT?

A PHOTOGRAPH-TAKER.
ONE OF THOSE... "CAMERAS"?
THAT'S ANOTHER NAME FOR THEM, YEAH. ANYWAY, USE IT HOWEVER YOU LIKE.

I GUESS IT'S A PRETTY OLD ONE.
KYU (TWIST)

HE TOLD US TO USE IT HOWEVER WE LIKE, BUT...?
OOH!

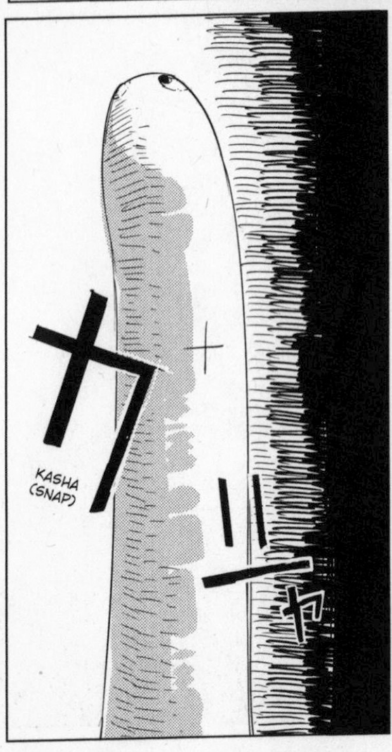
KASHA (SNAP)

KACHI (CLICK)
L-700
SHOOT. IT'S STILL BLURRY.
THERE ARE A LOT OF THOSE STATUES AROUND HERE, HUH?
WONDER WHAT THEY ARE.
THEY LOOK KINDA LIKE YOUR FACE, CHII-CHAN.
THEY DO NOT.
HEY! LOOK!
WHAT?
PASHA (SNAP)
NO GOOD. BLURRY AGAIN.

CAMERA: TSUKISHIMA PRECISION INSTRUMENTS

CHII-CHAN, LOOK THIS WAY ONE MORE TIME.
LOOK, YOU... I HAVE TO KEEP MY EYES ON THE ROAD WHEN I'M DRIVING.

IT'LL BE FIIIINE.

ZU (LOOM)
AH...

GO (KONK)

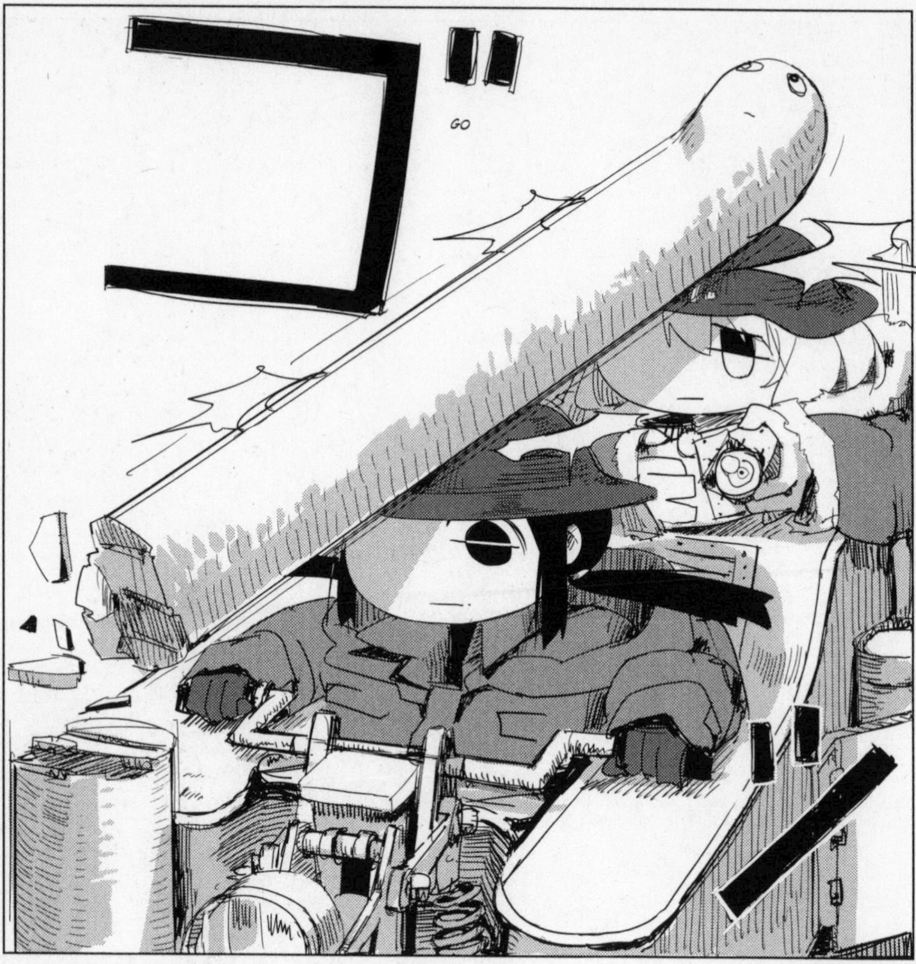

GO

JIIII
(KRRK)

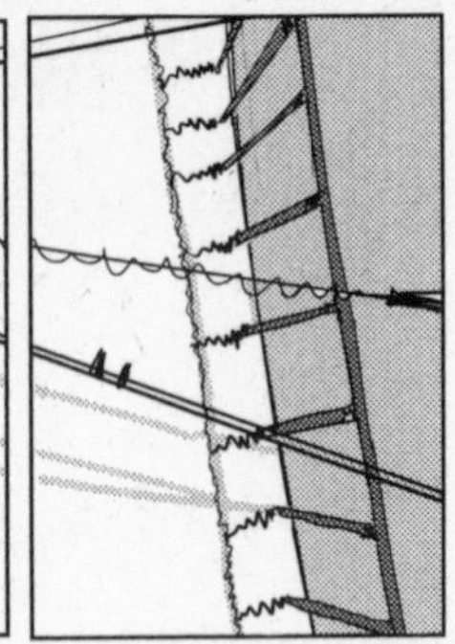

OWW...

ペチペチ
PECHI (SMACK)
PECHI

SHEEEESH. DON'T YOU KNOW YOU GOTTA KEEP YOUR EYES ON THE ROAD WHEN YOU'RE DRIVING?
ぺしぺし
PESHI (PAT)
PESHI

BASHI (THWACK)
OW!

I'LL BE HOLDING ON TO THIS.
AWW ...

GEEEEZ. YOU'RE HEARTLESS, CHII-CHAN.
カチカチカチカチ
SFX: KACHI (CLICK) KACHI KACHI KACHI

IF ONLY YOUR HEART WERE AS BIG AS THAT STATUE.
KASHA (SNAP)
HUH?

WHAT WAS THAT? THE SHUTTER WENT OFF BY ITSELF.
YUU, DID YOU TOUCH ANY-THING?
I MIGHT HAVE PRESSED A BUTTON WHEN WE CRASHED.

MAYBE THIS...
KARI (KRIK)
KARI
KARI

WHAT IS IT?
I THINK I'M STARTING TO FIGURE OUT WHAT THE DIALS DO.

OOOH, TELL ME, TELL ME!
TOTOTOTOTO (PUTTER)
NO.

IF WE KEEP GOING LIKE THIS...

...WE SHOULD REACH THAT BIG, BRIGHT BUILDING SOON.

MOGU (MUNCH)
モグ
SURE TOOK A LOT OF PHOTOS...
LIKE, A STUPID AMOUNT ...
ARE YOU STILL MAD?
I'M NOT MAD.

カチ
KACHI (CLICK)
カチ
KACHI
YUU, YOU TOOK TOO MANY OF THAT WEIRD STATUE.
SO WHAT? IT'S NOT LIKE IT'LL RUN OUT OF PICTURES.

IT WILL EVENTU-ALLY...
IT WILL?

HOW MANY MORE D'YOU THINK WE CAN TAKE?
IT'S PROBABLY THIS NUMBER HERE...

I'M THINKING THIS IS THE NUMBER OF PHOTOS REMAINING.
IT'S BEEN GOING DOWN LITTLE BY LITTLE SINCE WE STARTED TAKING THEM.

1/4000
520014
FIVE HUN-DRED TWENTY THOU-SAND.

HOW MANY MORE DAYS' WORTH OF PROVISIONS DO WE HAVE AGAIN?
MOSU (NIBBLE)
もす
BETWEEN THE TWO OF US, WE'RE SET FOR ABOUT THIRTY DAYS.

I DON'T SEE US USING UP THAT MANY PHOTOS BEFORE THEN...
IF I HAD TO, I COULD EAT UP ALL OF THE FOOD BY MYSELF IN SEVEN DAYS.
DON'T YOU DARE.

OH.
CHII-CHAN, THIS SAYS TODAY'S FOOD IS CHEESE-FLAVORED.
WHAT EVEN IS CHEESE ...?
CHEESE ...
MOGU (MUNCH)
モグモグ...
MOGU

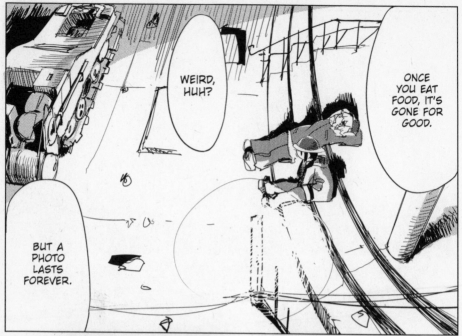

ONCE YOU EAT FOOD, IT'S GONE FOR GOOD.

WEIRD, HUH?

BUT A PHOTO LASTS FOREVER.

EVEN IF SOMEDAY THE CITY COLLAPSES AND ALL THOSE STATUES CRUMBLE AWAY...

...THEY'LL LIVE ON IN PHOTOS. IT'S A NICE THOUGHT.
......

I KNOW... THAT FUNCTION I FOUND EARLIER...
パカ
PAKA (CLACK)
TURN THIS AND...

STAY RIGHT THERE.
?

SFX: KACHI (CLICK) KACHI KACHI KACHI KACHI KACHI KACHI KACHI

カチカチカチカチカチカチカチカチ

KASHA (SNAP)

3230.08.06.21.04

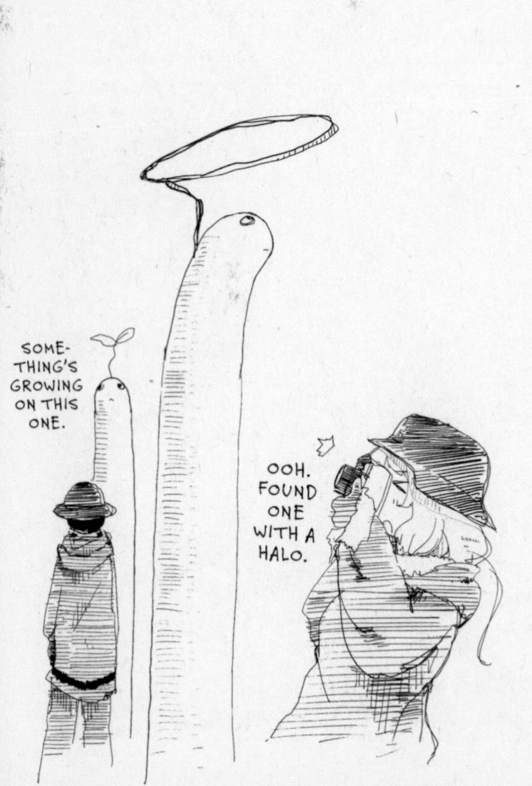
SOME-
THING'S
GROWING
ON THIS
ONE.
OOH.
FOUND
ONE
WITH A
HALO.

SFX: TOTOTOTOTO (PUTTER)

THAT EXTRA-BRIGHT BUILDING...
GI (SQUEAK)

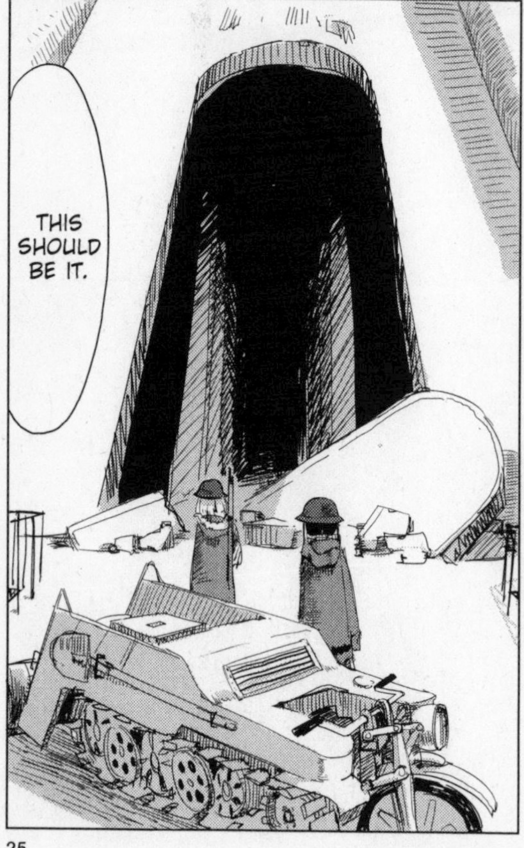
THIS SHOULD BE IT.

WHEN WE SAW IT AT NIGHT, IT WAS BRIGHT...

...BUT IT'S TOTALLY DARK INSIDE.

パチ
PACHI (PCHK)
SO LARGE.
WHAT KIND OF FACILITY WAS IT...?
カッ
KA
カッ
KA (KLAK)

THERE ARE SO MANY BIG STATUES.
THE WEIRD ONE AGAIN?

I THINK THIS MIGHT BE A TEMPLE.
KOTSU (TOK)
コッ
KATSU (TAK)
カッ

A TEMPLE?
KOTSU
コッ
KATSU
カッ
A PLACE WHERE THE GODS LIVE.
KATSU
カッ

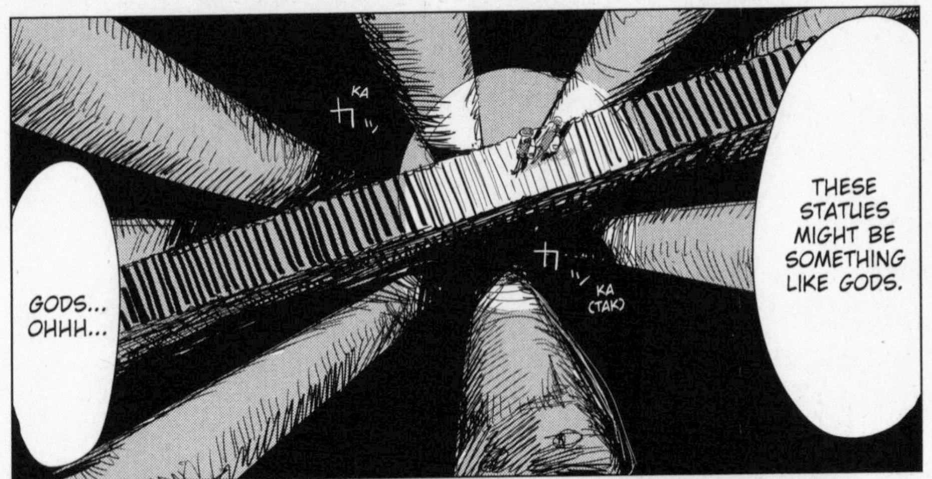
THESE STATUES MIGHT BE SOMETHING LIKE GODS.
KA
カッ
カッ
KA (TAK)
GODS... OHHH...

WHAT'S A "GOD"?
GODS ARE...

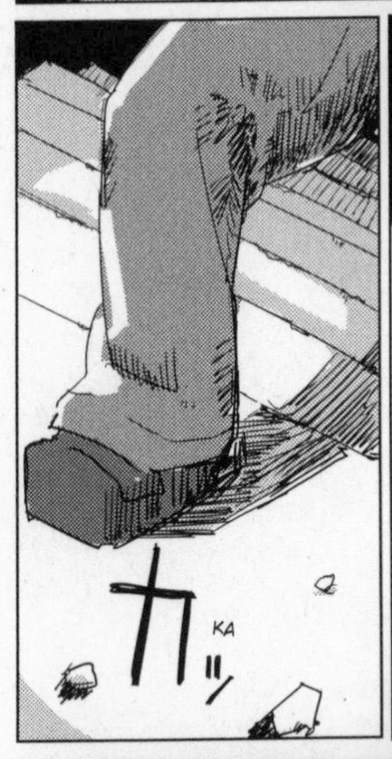
カッ
KA

HMM... WHAT ARE THEY?
カッ
KA
カッ
KA

THERE'S WRITING ON THIS...
ERECTED ABOUT FOUR HUNDRED YEARS AGO... DEDICATED TO THREE GODS...

I WAS RIGHT. LOOKS LIKE IT'S A TEMPLE.
HUH...

"HEAV-
EN"...
IT SAYS THIS TEMPLE WAS MADE IN THE IMAGE OF THE AFTER-LIFE.

HEAV-
EN...

IT TALKS ABOUT GODS TOO.
"BEINGS WHO ILLUMINATE THE AFTERLIFE."

THAT'S PRETTY VAGUE...

ヂヂヂヂヂ
JIJIJIJIJI (FIZZLE)
ボッ
BO (BWFF)

HUH?
FU (FFFT)

DID I FORGET TO TOP OFF THE FUEL...?

FU

WHA—? CHII-CHAN...?

IT'S PITCH-BLACK...

CHII-CHAN, WHERE ARRRE YOUUU?
YUU. OVER HERE.
OVER WHERE?

...HEY, CHII-CHAN? BEING SEPARATED IN THE DARK...
YUU?
...IS KINDA SCARY, ISN'T IT?

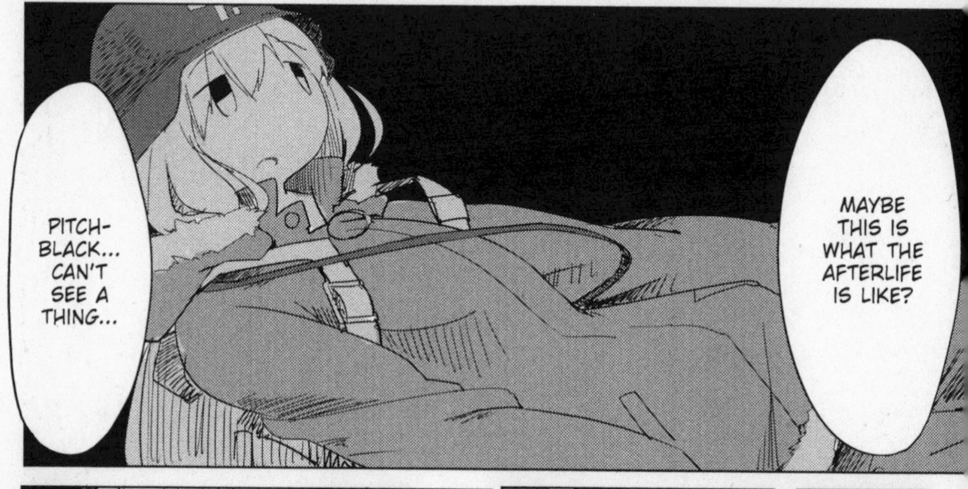
MAYBE THIS IS WHAT THE AFTERLIFE IS LIKE?
PITCH-BLACK... CAN'T SEE A THING...

GON (KONK)
OW!
OH!

HUH? IS THIS YOUR FACE?
PETA (PAT)

NO...
PA (FLASH)
LIGHT...
AH!

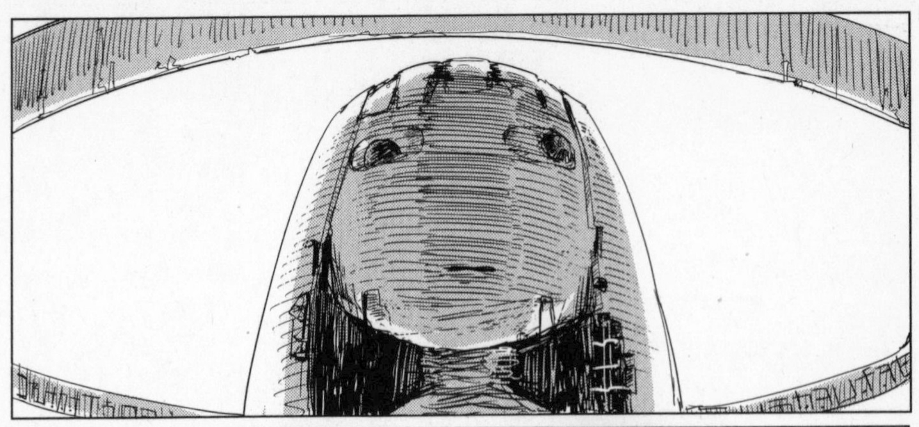

......

A BEING THAT LIGHTS UP THE DARK...

EVEN THE FLOOR LOOKS LIKE IT'S SHINING.
IT'S REFLECT-ING THE LIGHT.
THESE ARE... REPLICA PLANTS, MAYBE?

スリ...
SURI (RUB)
MADE OF METAL ...?

CHII-CHAN! LOOK!
WHAT?

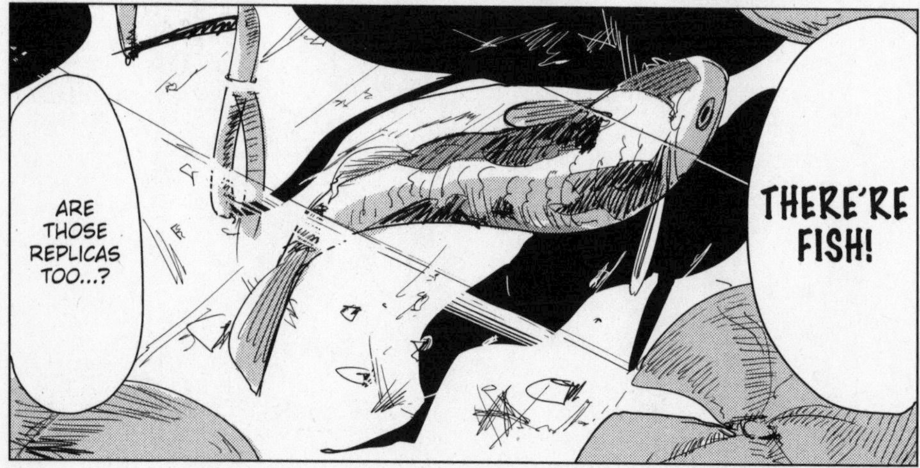
THERE'RE FISH!
ARE THOSE REPLICAS TOO...?

"REH-PLI-CUH" ...?
DOES THAT MEAN WE CAN'T EAT IT?
USE YOUR EYES.

IT'S ENCASED IN GLASS.
ALMOST LIKE THE SURFACE OF WATER...
SURI (TOUCH)
スリ...
WHAT A LET-DOWN...
THE GODS ARE A LET-DOWN...
THESE THINGS ARE JUST PLAIN OLD STATUES.

BE CAREFUL WHAT YOU SAY, OR YOU'LL GET PUNISHED.
DIVINE JUDGMENT.
BUT DIDN'T YOU KNOCK OVER ONE OF THE STATUES ON OUR WAY HERE?

...THAT THING WAS JUST A PLAIN OLD STATUE.
I KNEW IT.

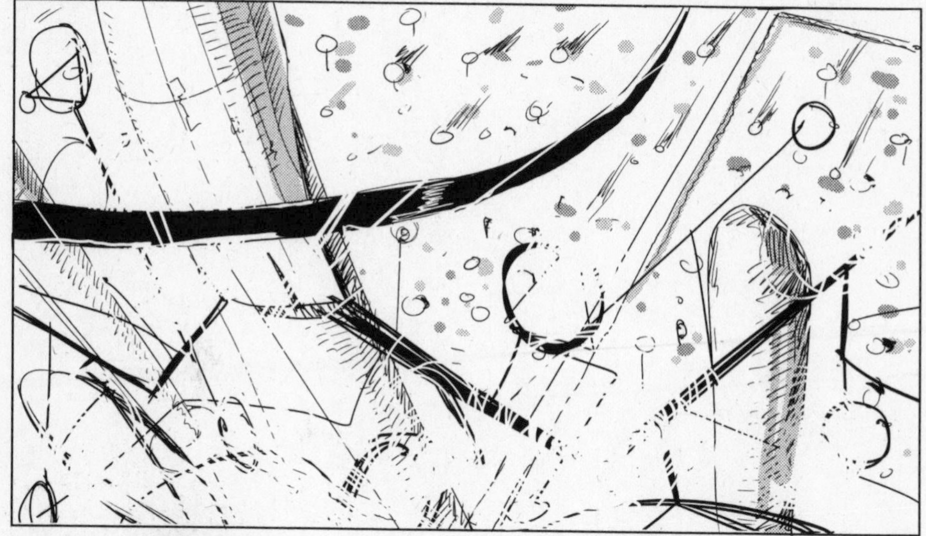
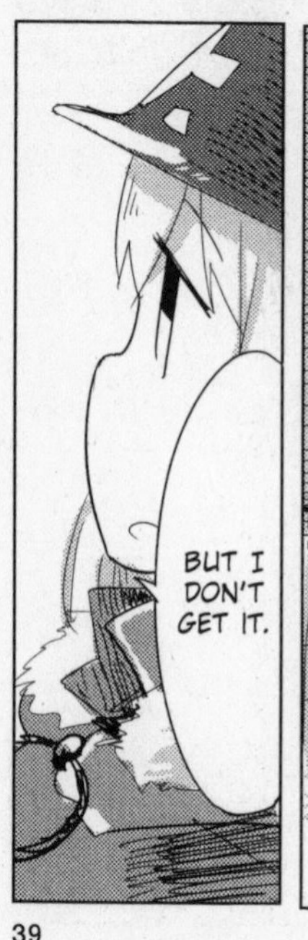
BUT I DON'T GET IT.

RATIONS WITH A SIDE OF THE AFTERLIFE ARE PRETTY TASTY.
YUM.

ULTIMATELY, THESE GREAT GODS ARE JUST IMITATIONS TOO, RIGHT?

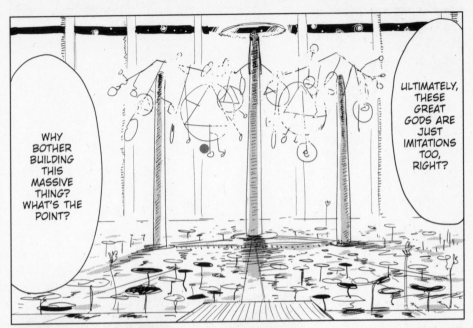

WHY BOTHER BUILDING THIS MASSIVE THING? WHAT'S THE POINT?

NOBODY ACTUALLY KNOWS ANYTHING ABOUT THE AFTERLIFE.
HMM...

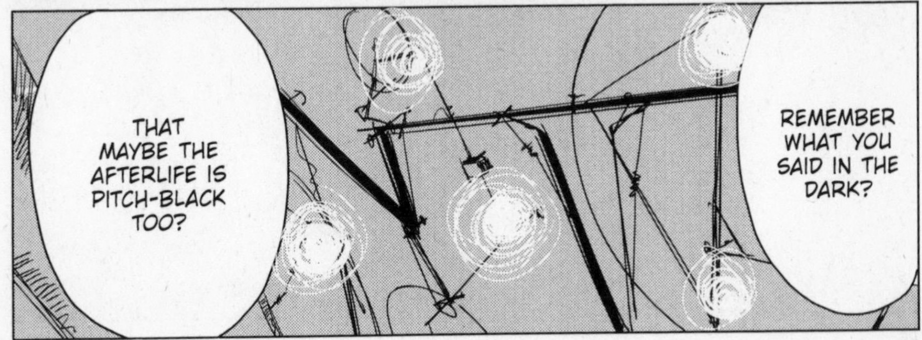
REMEMBER WHAT YOU SAID IN THE DARK?
THAT MAYBE THE AFTERLIFE IS PITCH-BLACK TOO?

MAYBE PEOPLE BUILD STATUES AND TURN ON LIGHTS...
...BECAUSE THEY DON'T WANT TO THINK THAT.
FOR PEACE OF MIND.
PEACE OF MIND, HUH...?
モグ…
MOGU (MNCH)

BUT I GOT MORE PEACE OF MIND WHEN I FOUND YOU...

...IN THE DARK.

AH!

COULD IT BE THAT YOU'RE A GOD...?

YUU, DID YOU KNOW...

...YOU HAVE TO OFFER FOOD TO GODS AS TRIBUTE?
GIMME.
AH, I MUST HAVE BEEN MISTAKEN AFTER ALL.

AH! BETTER YET, I COULD BE A GOD.
AS IF.

PASHA
(SNAP)
パシャ
I AM A GOD...

11 RESIDENCE

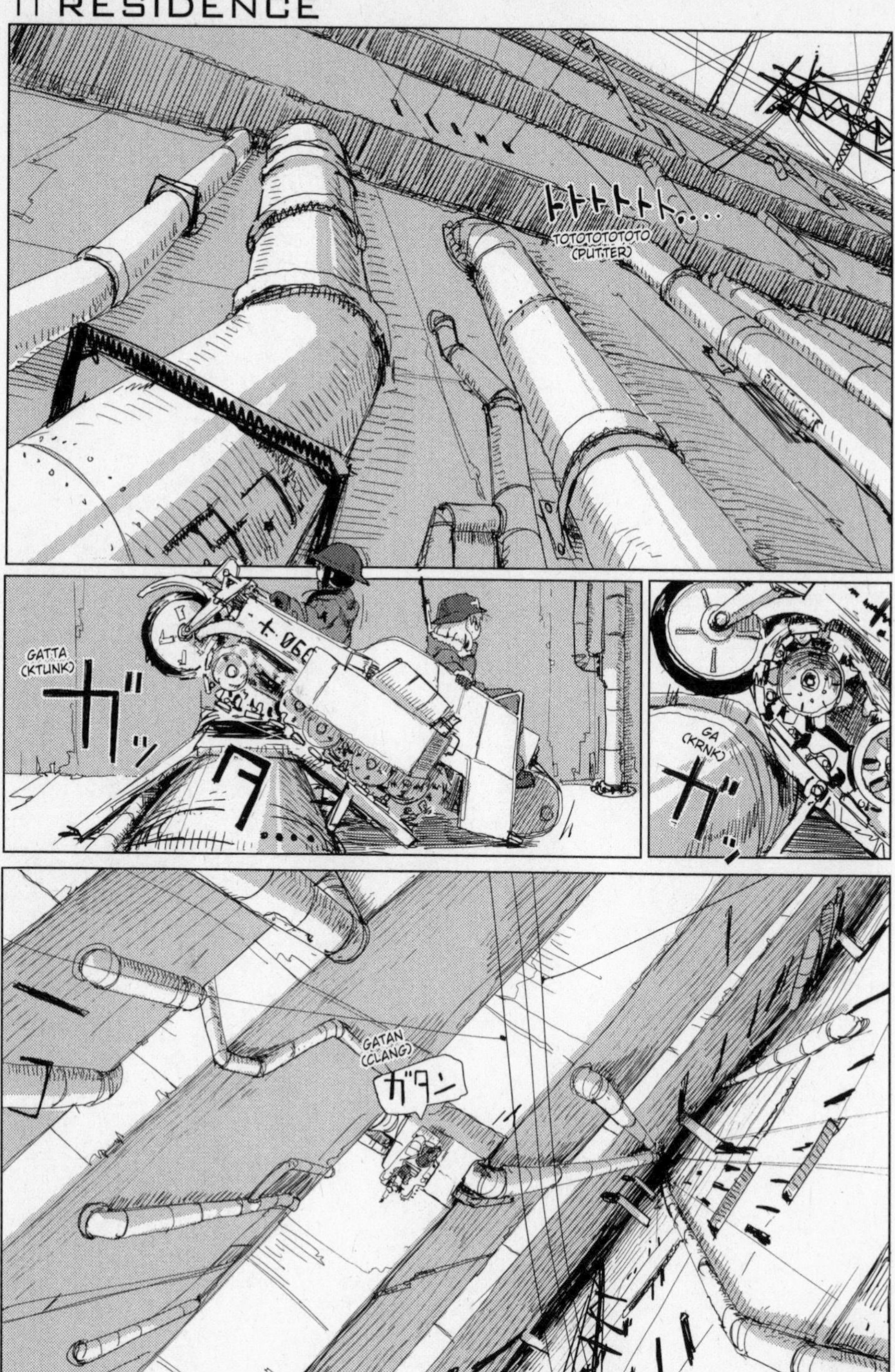

トトトトトト…
TOTOTOTOTOTO (PUTTER)
ガッタ…
GATTA (KTUNK)
ガガ
GA (KRNK)
ガタン
GATAN (CLANG)

NNNNNN
(CLANG)
TOTOTOTOTO
(PUTTER)

THE POWER AND WATER LINES ARE PRETTY INTACT...
トトトトト
TOTOTOTOTO

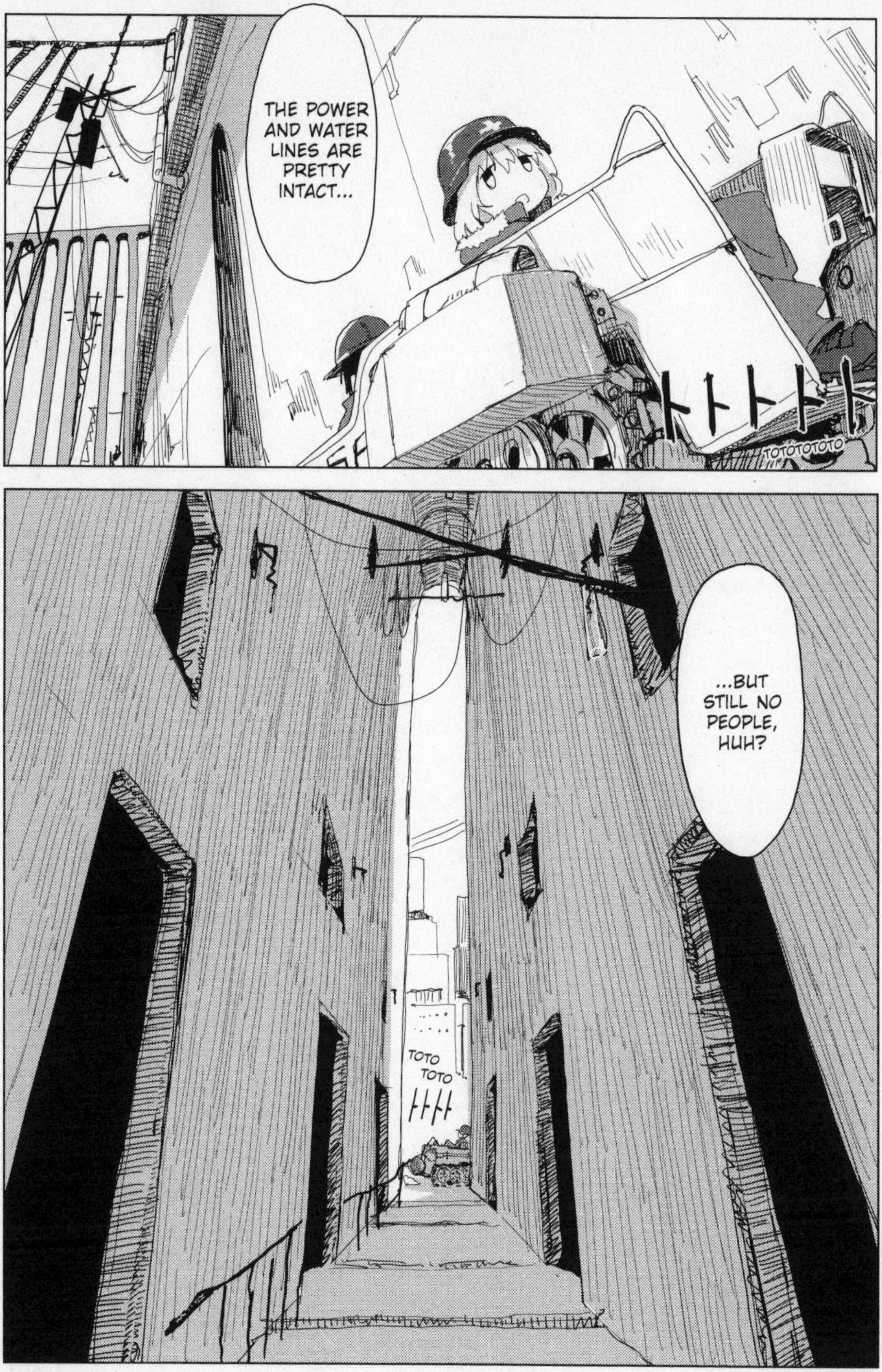

...BUT STILL NO PEOPLE, HUH?

TOTO TOTO

トトトト

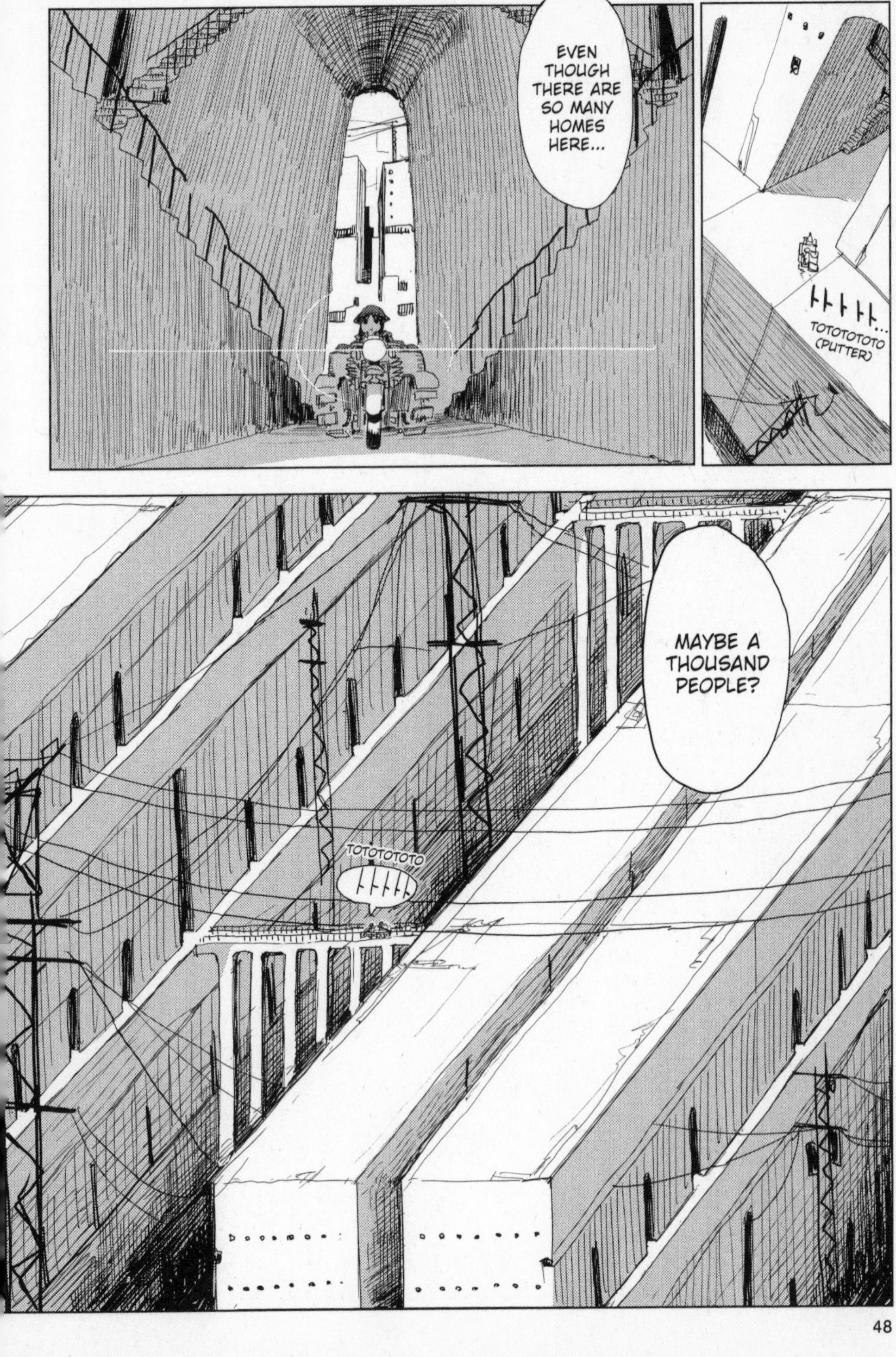

トトトトト…
TOTOTOTOTO (PUTTER)
EVEN THOUGH THERE ARE SO MANY HOMES HERE...

MAYBE A THOUSAND PEOPLE?
TOTOTOTOTO
トトトトト

MUST HAVE BEEN A BUNCH OF PEOPLE LIVING HERE...
トトトトト....
TOTOTOTOTO
HOW MANY DOES THAT MEAN?

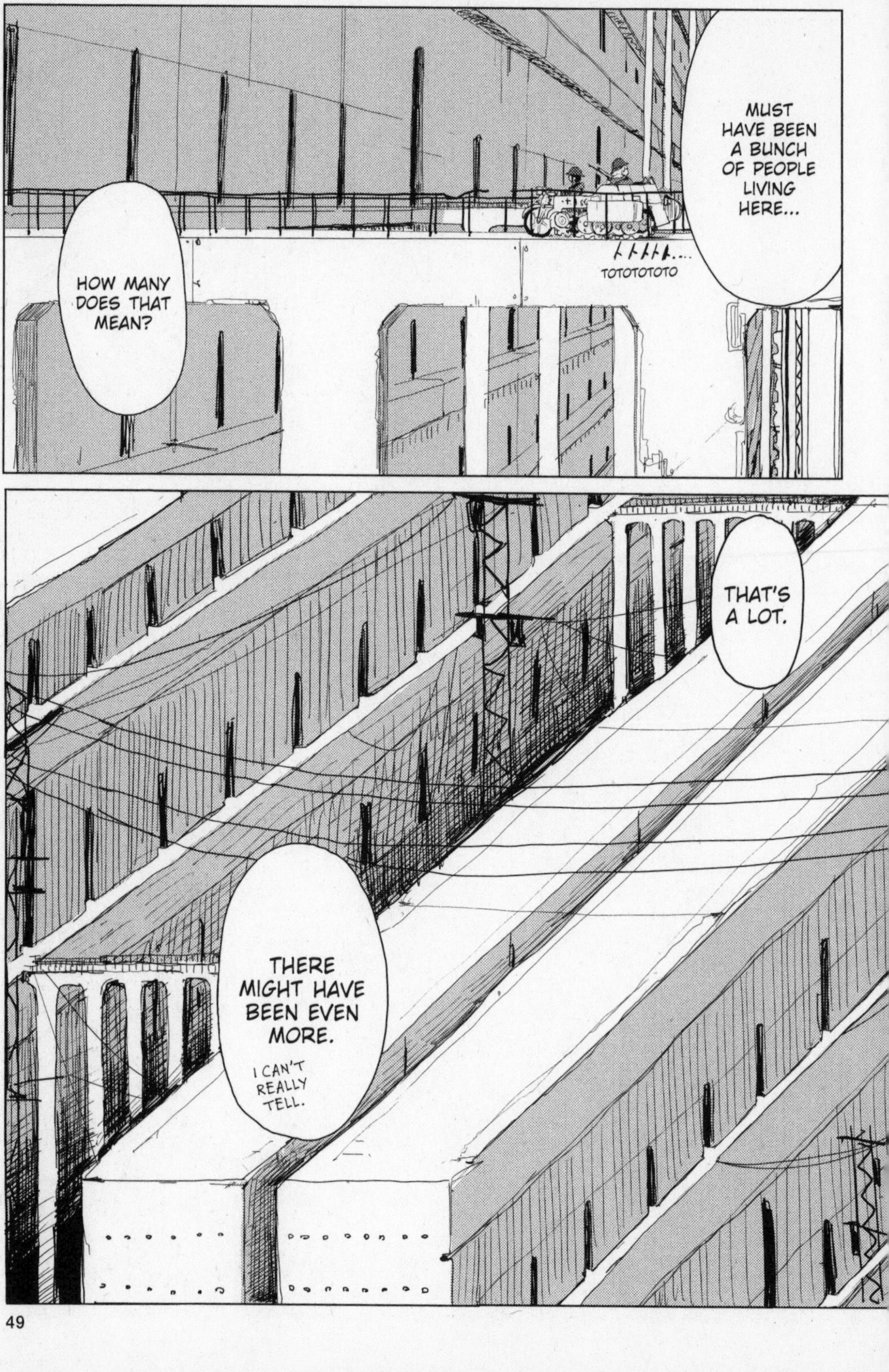

THAT'S A LOT.

THERE MIGHT HAVE BEEN EVEN MORE.

I CAN'T REALLY TELL.

KOTSU
コツ....
KOTSU (TOK)
コツ....
HEY...

...WHAT ARE HOMES FOR AGAIN?
WITHOUT A HOME, YOU HAVE NOWHERE TO LIVE.

BUT WE DON'T HAVE A HOME.
THAT'S TRUE ENOUGH ...

HEY, DOES THAT COUNT?

HMM?

OUR VEHICLE.

YOU KNOW THAT'S NOT A HOME.

ANSWER "YES" OR "NO."

...NO.

'COS THERE'S "NO" PLACE LIKE HOME?

CRAM IT.

WELL, WE DID HAVE ONE OF OUR OWN ONCE... A HOME...

...BUT IT'S GONE NOW...
HUH?

THIS ROOM HAS A DOOR.
YOU'RE RIGHT.

GACHA (KCHAK)

ギィ…
GII (CREAK)
THERE ARE THINGS INSIDE.
IT'S A PRETTY NEAT ROOM, HUH?
キュ
KYU (SQUIK)
THERE'S RUNNING WATER TOO...
ジョロっ….
JORO (SPLOSH)
OOH.
I LIKE THESE CHAIRS.

とっ
TO (PLOP)

AHH... THAT'S A NICE VIEW...

THE SUN'S GOTTEN PRETTY LOW TOO.

MAKES ME WISH WE COULD JUST LIVE HERE.
THEN WHY DON'T WE?

HUH? CAN WE?
IT'S KIND OF A DREAM OF MINE, YOU KNOW?
LIVING IN A PLACE LIKE THIS.
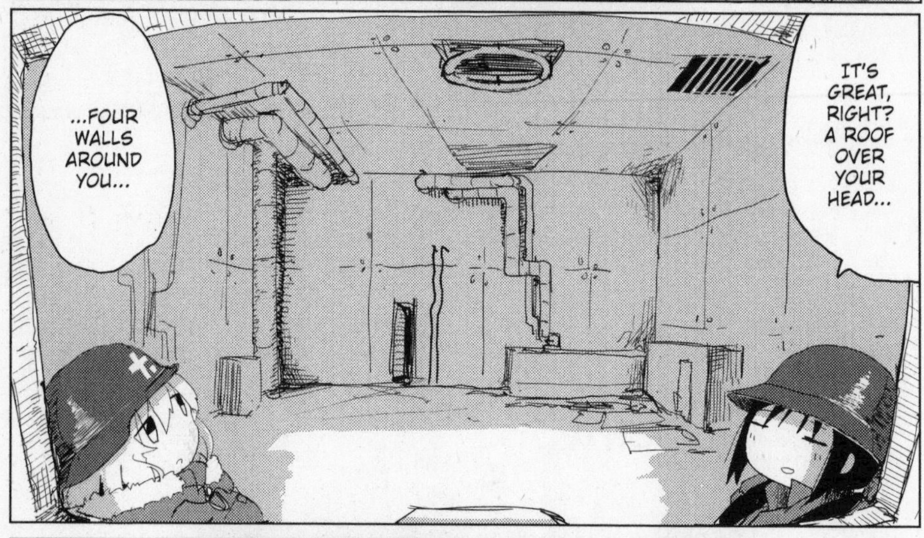
IT'S GREAT, RIGHT? A ROOF OVER YOUR HEAD...
...FOUR WALLS AROUND YOU...

IF WE'RE GOING TO LIVE HERE, I WANT ONE OF THOSE, UM, YOU KNOW... A BED.
OH YEAH? A BED?

I SAW ONE FOR TWO PEOPLE IN A BOOK ONCE. A DOUBLE-BUNK BED.
LIKE THIS.
I WANT THAAAT.
OOH, THAT'S A GOOD IDEA.

I'D PUT IT OVER THERE.
ALL RIGHT, THEN I'D WAAANT... BOOK-SHELVES.

WHAT'S THAT?
USE YOUR BRAIN. THEY'RE SHELVES WITH BOOKS ON THEM.
I SAW THOSE IN A BOOK TOO.
LOTS OF BOOKS...
???

THEN I WANT FOOD-SHELVES!
WHAT'S THAT?
SHELVES STUFFED FULL WITH FOOD.

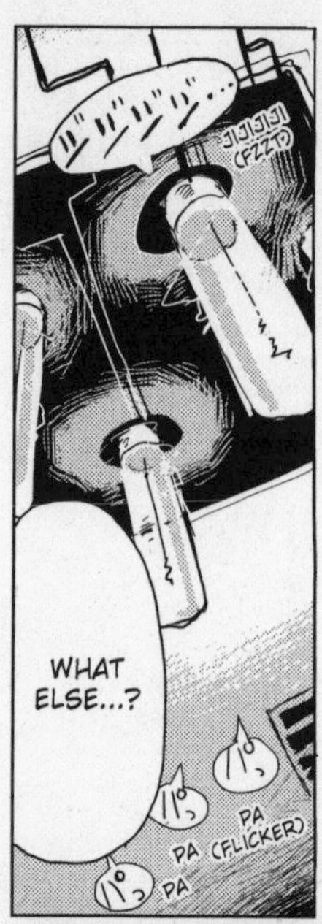
ジジジジ…
JIJIJIJI (FZZT)
WHAT ELSE...?
パッ
パッ
パッ
PA
PA (FLICKER)
PA

I WANT A HEATER.
LIKE A STOVE.
AND A BATHTUB.
I GUESS THE PEOPLE OF OLD DECORATED THEIR HOMES WITH PLANTS AND SO ON TOO.
I'D LIKE TO TRY THAT.
WE SHOULD PUT IN A STATUE TOO.
NO THANKS.
パッ
PA

SURE WOULD BE NICE...

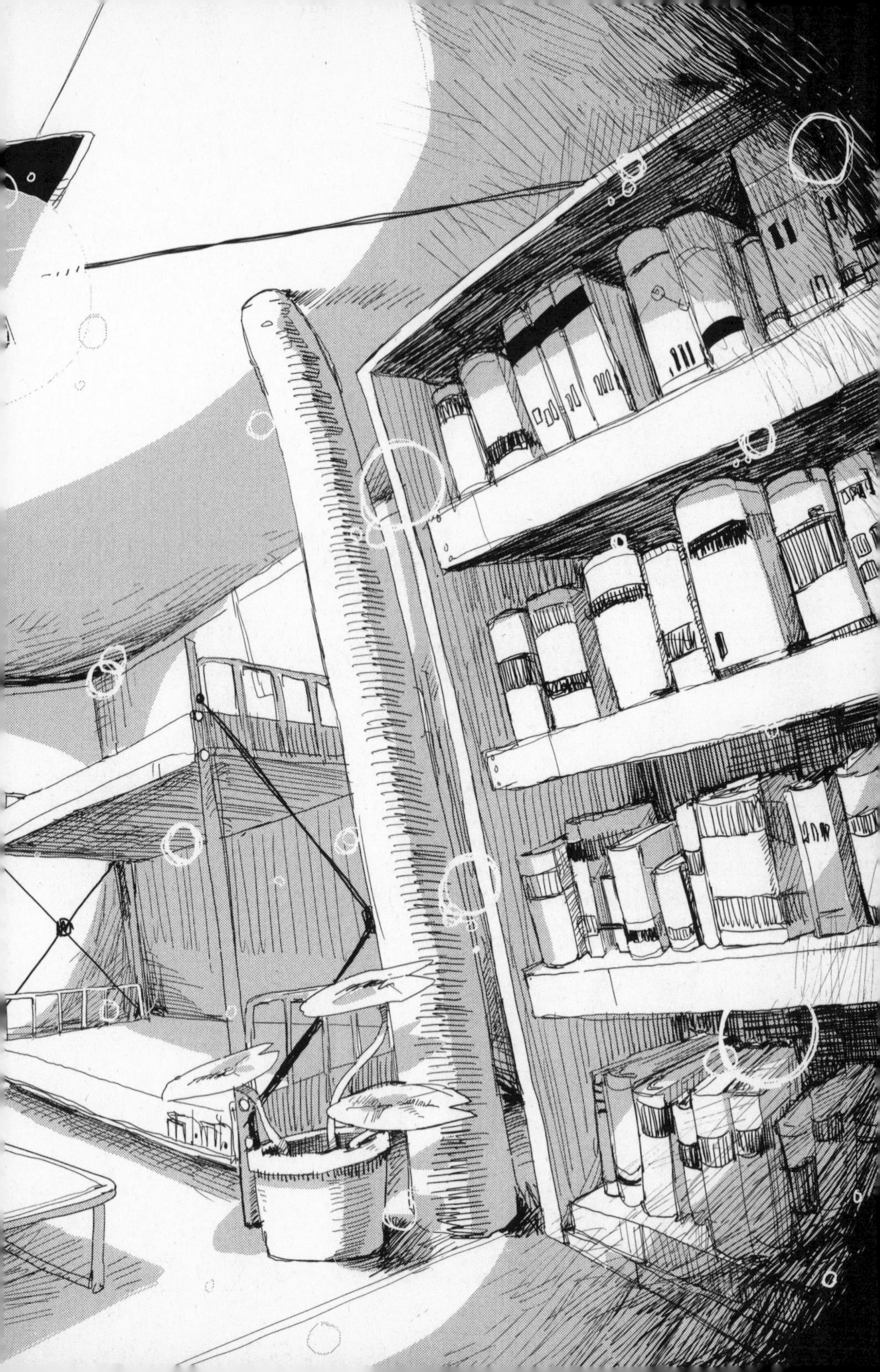

...THAT WOULD BE INCREDIBLE.

BUT IF WE STICK AROUND HERE, OUR FOOD'LL RUN OUT IN NO TIME.

...IT'S PRETTY LATE. LET'S STAY HERE FOR THE NIGHT.

—WHEN ALL'S SAID AND DONE...
...IT'S ALWAYS BACK TO THE CYCLE OF RESUPPLYING AND MOVING ON FOR US...

GUESS THAT MEANS THE ROAD IS OUR HOME.
IT'S A LOVELY ROOFLESS HOME...
YAAAY.
GATAN (RATTLE)
TOTOTOTOTOTOTOTOTO (PAPUMPUMPUM)

OH, WHAT IF WE PUT A ROOF ON IT?
LIKE THIS...
WE DON'T NEED THAT...

12 NAP

FURA
FURA (SWERVE)
TOTOTOTOTO (PUTTER)

AAAAGH...

CAN'T GO ON. I'M TOO SLEEPY...
LET'S TAKE A BREAK. A BREEEAK.

WE WERE UP SO LATE LAST NIGHT...
SINCE IT WAS BRIGHT...
HEH, WE SURE GOT CARRIED AWAY YESTERDAY.
I DON'T KNOW IF I'D SAY THAT...

コト
KOTO
(KAKLAK)

YOUR TURN, CHII-CHAN.
KUH!

プルプル
PURU
PURU
(TREMBLE)

フー
FUU
(FWOOOO)

グラッ
GURA
(SWAY)

AAAAAAAH!
GARA (CLATTER)

HEY! DID YOU JUST BLOW ON IT?
MUST'VE BEEN A BREEZE.

GRR...
HOW MANY WINS AM I AT NOW? TEN?

FINE, WE'LL PLAY ONE MORE TIME.
HEY, WANNA BET ONE OF TOMOR-ROW'S RATION STICKS?
OKAY, BUT NO CHEAT-ING.
I DIDN'T CHEAT.

I ENDED UP HAVING TO GIVE YUU ONE OF MY STICKS...

SHE'S AL-READY OUT LIKE A LIGHT.

オオオオオ…ン…
OOOOON (VRMMMM)

パチ
PACHI (BLINK)
GURA (SWAY)

THE GROUND'S SHAKING...
AN EARTH-QUAKE?
GURA
GURA
BA (BOLT)

グラ
GURA
グラ
GURA (SWAY)
WHOA ...
HOW'D I GET UP HERE?

グラ
GURA
グラ
GURA

CHII-CHAN! CHII-CHAN!

YUU?

YOU OKAY?
YOU'RE HUGE!
ZUZUUN (THOOOOM)
ズズーン

GA (CRUNCH)
ガッ
WAH! IDIOT! DON'T MOVE!
IT'S NOT STABLE!
ZUZUUN
ズズ…ン

LISTEN TO ME, YUU. IF THIS THING FALLS OVER, I'LL—
CUT IT OUT!
FUU (FWOOO)
GURA (WOBBLE)

WHOOOA...!

WHOA...

WHAT'RE YOU DANCING FOR?
WHY, YOU...
GURA

LISTEN CLOSELY, OKAY? I NEED YOU TO PICK ME UP VERY CAREFULLY...

HEY!
FUU

HA HA HA HA HA HA HA HA!
TOO FUNNY.
YOUUUUU!
GARA (CLATTER)

YOU'LL REGRET THIS...!

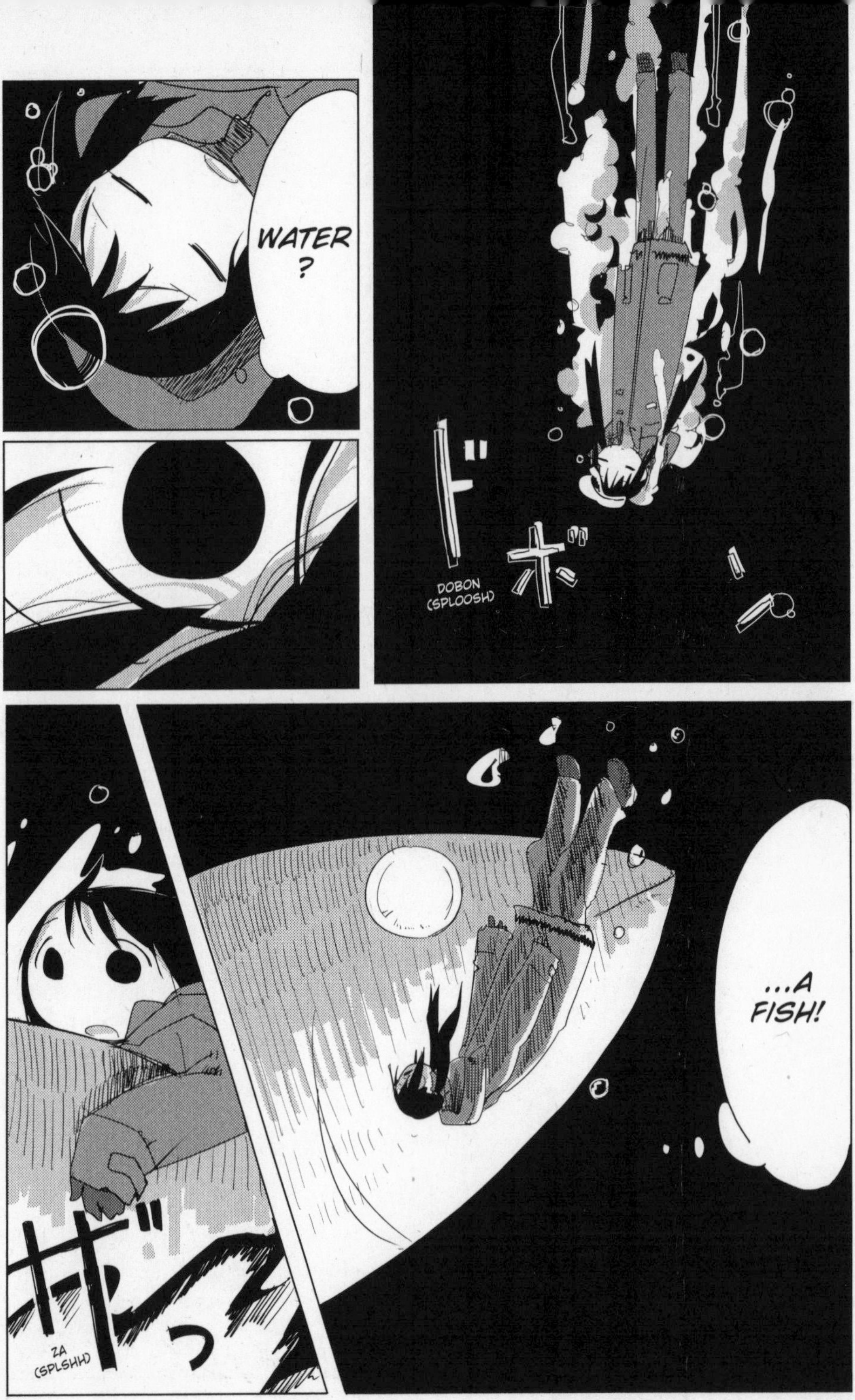

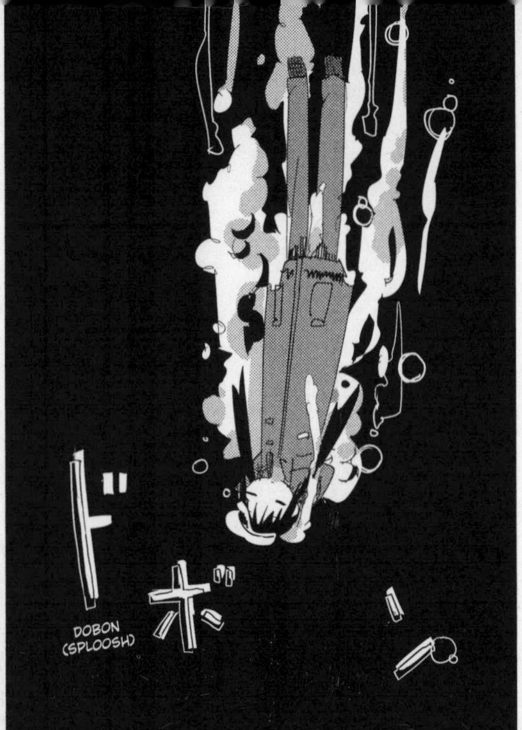
DOBON
(SPLOOSH)

WATER
?

...A
FISH!
ZA
(SPLSHH)

IS THIS...
ZAZAAN (FSHHH)
PASHA
PASHA (SPLISH)
... "OCEAN" ...?
WHOOOA...
THIS FISH...
IS IT THE ONE WE...?
ZAZAA
WHAT?
NOPE, NOT THAT ONE.
ZA
ZA
ZA
ZA
ZA

パ
ザブン
ZABUN
(SHLOSH)
YUU
!?

ZAPPA (SPLOOSH)

ZAPUN (SPLASH)
THAT'S RIGHT.
YOU'RE HUGE.

THE FISH FROM LAUNDRY DAY IS THIS ONE HERE.
BOOOONES...
チャプ CHAPU (SLOSH)
チャプ CHAPU
RIGHT, 'COS WE ATE IT...

THAT FISH TASTED SO GOOD...
YOU'RE A FISH TOO, AREN'T YOU?
YOU LOOK LIKE YOU'D TASTE GOOD TOO, CHII-CHAN.
ズ ZU (LOOM)
HAVE YOU LOST YOUR MIND?

HEY, I'M JUST A FISH.
ザバッ ZA (SPLASH)
WHOA! WAIT!

STOPPP!

SHE'S GONNA EAT ME...

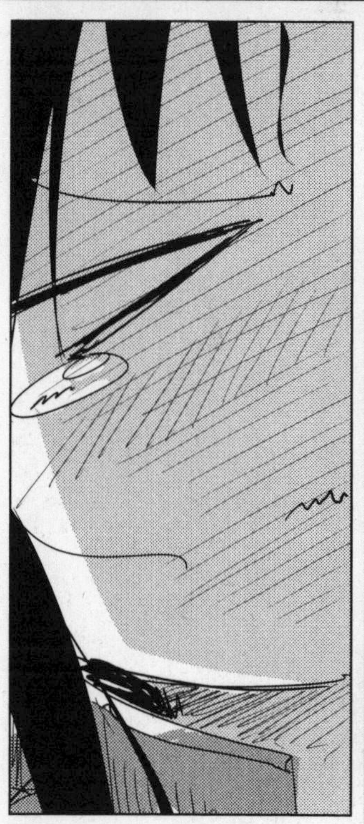

AH!

OOOOOON
(OMM)
オオオオオオ……ン……

GUUU
(SNOOORE)
グ~~…
BIKU
(FLINCH)
ビクッ

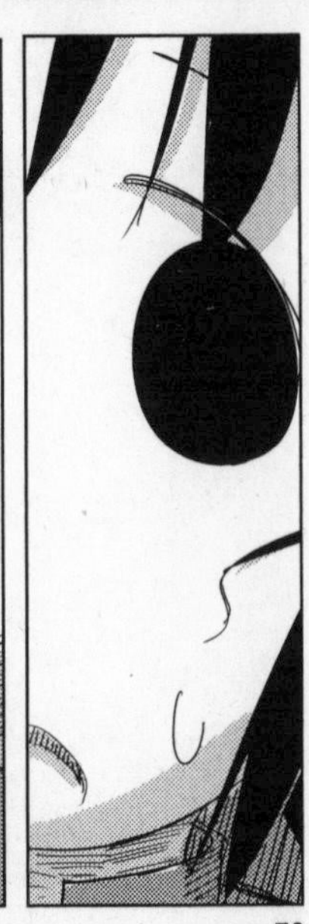

MNYAH... I CAN'T EAT ANOTHER BITE...
イラッ
IRA (TWITCH)

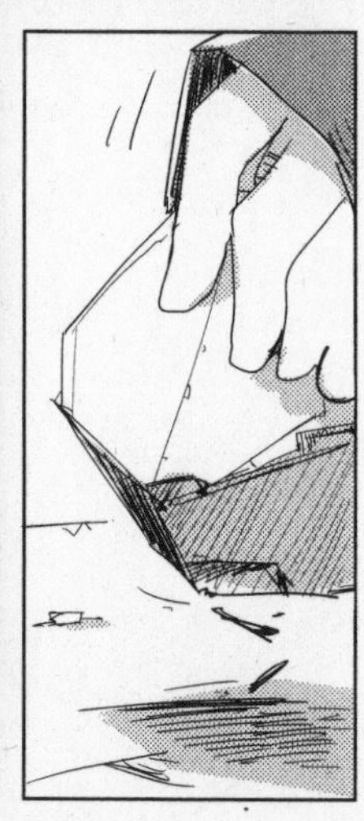

ガッ ガッ
GA
GA (SHOVE)
EAT ROCK.

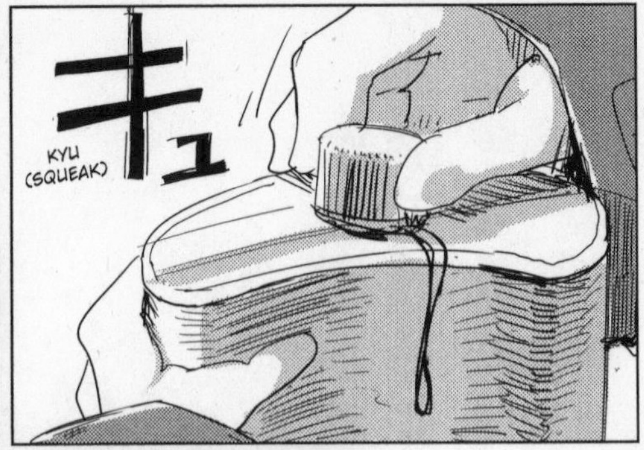
キュ
KYU (SQUEAK)

んっんっ…
N (GULP)
N

PWAH!
I FEEL LIKE I WENT ON A LONG, WEIRD JOURNEY…

THE WATER'S DELI-CIOUS.

GRGH …

MMRGH NH
MGMRRTH...!
(THERE'S A
ROCK IN MY
MOUTH!!)
NHHH...

GIRLS' LAST TOUR

13

13 RAIN SONG

NH.
TOTOTOTO (PUTTER)
TOTOTOTO
トトトト トトトト……

……
PLIP

CHII-CHAN…
WHAT?

TTAAAAN (CLONGGG)

TATATAN (TATATAMM)
TOTOTON (TUTUTUMM)

ZAAA (FSHHH)

RAAAAAAIN!

ZAAA

IS THIS REALLY THE TIME TO GET EXCITED?

ZAAAAAAAAA

WHY CAN'T IT RAIN WHEN WE HAVE A ROOF OVER OUR HEADS?

WE NEED TO FIND SHELTER...

PULL THE TARP OVER OUR CARGO.

ZAAAAAAAAAAA

ROGER.

TO (PUTT)

TO

TO

TO

ZAAAAAA
(FSHHHHH)

SFX: TOTOTOTOTOTOTO (PUTTER)

WE GOT PRETTY SOAKED...

BASA (FLAP)

LET'S DRY THESE.

OH, FOUND SOME GOOD POLES.

HASN'T RAINED IN AGES.
YEAH.

IT'S SO LOUD...

ZAAAA

TON (PLIP)
TO TO TO
ZAAA (FSHHH)

BORRRED...
POLE.

KAAN (TAAANG)
KAAN
OOH, NEAT SOUND ...

THAT HAS A NICE RING TO IT. WONDER WHY.
KAAN
KAAN
KAAN
STOP BANGING THAT AROUND.

KON (TONK)
KON
IT'S PROB-ABLY HOLLOW.
WHEN SOMETHING'S EMPTY INSIDE, THE SOUND ECHOES IN IT.
OH, I SEE...

KON
KON
KON
KON
OOH, NEAT SOUND! MAYBE IT'S HOLLOW??
OW! OW!

BASHII (THWACK)

GASHI (CATCH)

LESS HOLLOW THAN YOURS, AT LEAST ...
PESHI (WHAP)
PESHI
GUEHH...
IF YOU HAVE NOTHING BETTER TO DO, GO FILL THE WATER BARREL.
'KAY.

GOOD GRIEF. ALWAYS SO QUICK TO HIT ME.
CHORORO (DRIBBLE)

IS HERE GOOD?
CHORO
CHORO

POCHIIN (PLINK)
POCHIIN
CHIRO (DIBBLE)
CHIRO
CHIRO

トロトロトロ...
TORO (THRM) TORO TORO TORO
KO (CLONK)

TAAN (CLONG)
TAAN

LET ME SEE YOUR HELMET.
SURE.

WHAT FOR?

TAAN (CLONG)
TAAN
TATAN (TATAM)
TATAN

OH. I THINK I LIKE THAT.
TATAAN
TATAAN
RIGHT ?

WANT TO TRY TO ADD MORE SOUNDS ...?
TAAAN
TAAAN
YEAH, THERE'S NO SHORTAGE OF LEAKS.

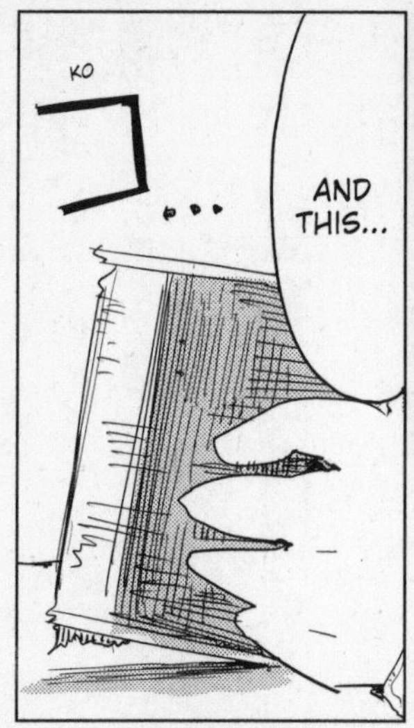
KO
コ…
AND THIS...

CHIIN (DING)
チーン

LOOK, LOOK!
I FOUND A WHOLE BUNCH OF CANS.

KAAN (TANGGG)
カーン

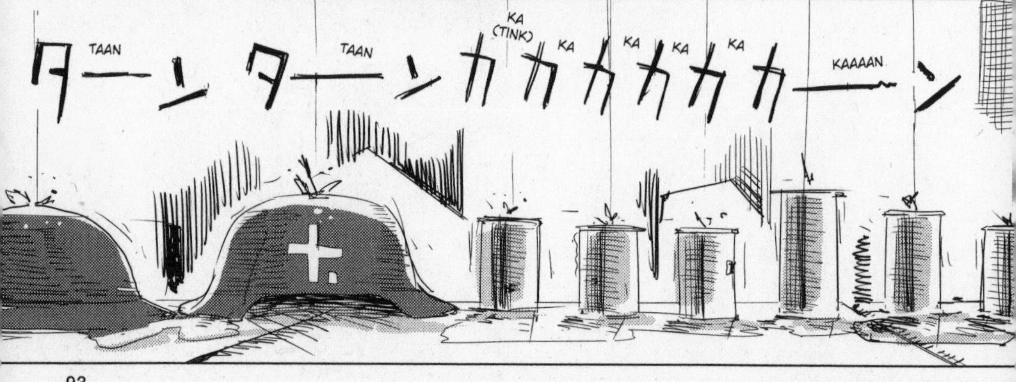
TAAN
ターン
TAAN
ターン
KA (TINK)
KA
KA
KA
KA
カカカカカーン
KAAAAN

TEN
KAN
CHIN (TING)
TON
KAN
TAN
TEN
TON
TATAN

CHIIIN
TAAAN (GONGGG)
KAN (TANG)
KAN
KAN
POTEN (PLINK
CHIIIN (DIIING)
TATAN
TOTOTON
TATEN (PIPANG)
KAN
KAN
TOTAN (POPING)
TETETE
TON (TNK)
TAAAN
TAN
KAKA (TAKKA)
KA
KAN
KO

IT'S LIKE A FLOOD OF SOUNDS, ISN'T IT?
CHIIIN (DING)
TAAN (GONG)
KAN
KAN
KAN (TANG)
KOON (KLONG)
TON
TON
TON (PONG)
TAN (TNK)
TAN
TAAN
TEN (PLINK)
TEN
I THINK...

...THIS MIGHT BE WHAT'S CALLED "MUSIC."
KAN
TAN
TOTE (DRIBBLE)
TO-
MUSIC ?

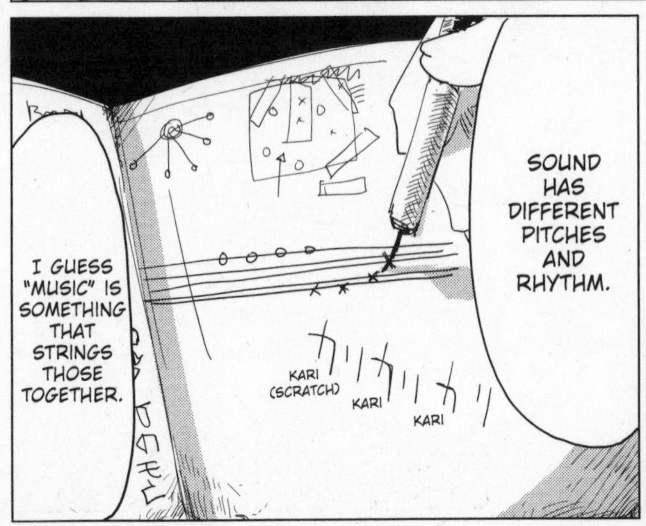
SOUND HAS DIFFERENT PITCHES AND RHYTHM.
I GUESS "MUSIC" IS SOMETHING THAT STRINGS THOSE TOGETHER.
KARI (SCRATCH)
KARI
KARI

KA
KA
KA

POCHI (PLIP)

MAYBE WE WENT A LITTLE OVER-BOARD.

KA

KA

KA

KA

KAAN

TAAAN

TAAAN

TAAN

TON

ZAAA (FSHH)

TON

TON

TEN

KAKAKAN

TEN

TAN

TA

TA

TA

TA

TE

AH.

THE RAIN ENDED ...

PICHI (DRIP)

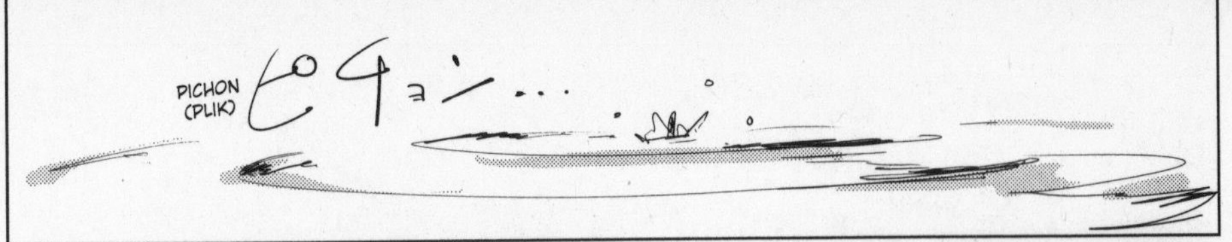
PICHON (PLIK)
ピチョン…

HEY, CHII-CHAN?

WAS THE WORLD ALWAYS SO...
SHE'S RIGHT...

IT'S SO QUIET...

LET'S REST HERE A BIT LONGER...
...
POCHAN (DRIP)
ポチャン…

GIRLS' LAST TOUR

14/15/16

14 BREAKDOWN

IT'S NO USE...
I CAN'T FIX IT...
GUNI (FWIP)
ぐにぐにぐに
GUNI
GUNI
THIS IS HOPE-LESS...
MMMNN... IT'S HOOOPE-LESSSS...
YUU, WILL YOU TAKE THAT BIT OF METAL OUT OF YOUR MOUTH AND HELP ME ALREADY?
HUUUH? DON'T WANNA.

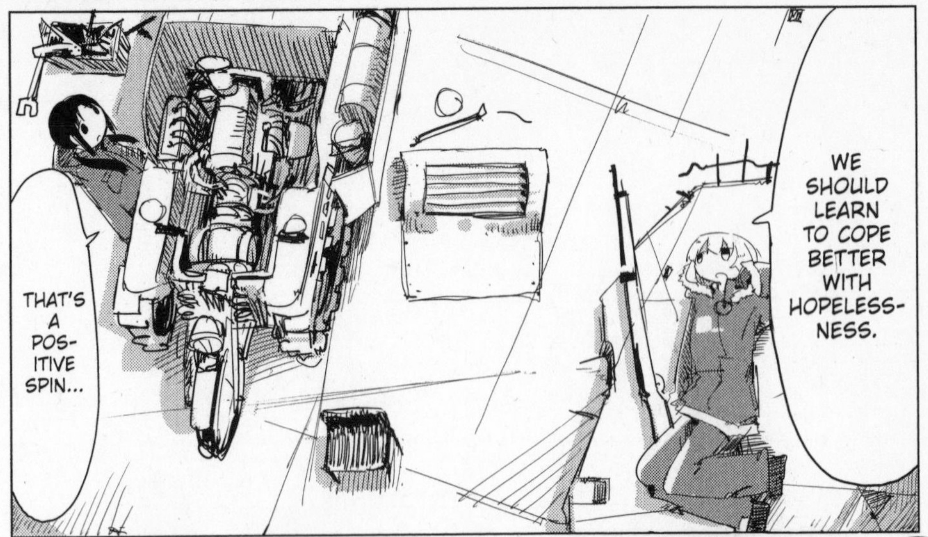
WE SHOULD LEARN TO COPE BETTER WITH HOPELESS-NESS.
THAT'S A POS-ITIVE SPIN...

カチャ
KACHA
カチャ
KACHA (CLANK)
WELL, WHATEVER. IF YOU TOUCHED IT, YOU'D ONLY BREAK IT WORSE ANYWAY...

WHAT DO I DO...?

IF WE DON'T FIX THIS...
...WE'LL BE STUCK HERE UNTIL WE...

C'MON, WHAT'S THE BIG DEAL?
WE DON'T HAVE TO GO ANYWHERE.

I GIVE UP! IT'S HOPE-LESS!

CHII-CHAN, LOOK AT THAT!

THERE!
NNNNN
(VRRRM)

IS THAT AN AIR-O-PLANE...?
AAAAH! YUU, LOOK!

A PERSON!

NO, I SAID THERE'S AN AIR-O-PLANE IN THE SKY!

WAIT, WHAT? WHERE?

AH! YOU'RE RIGHT. THERE'S SOME-THING FLYING...
AAAAH! LOOK! THERE'S A PERSON!!
I KNOW. I JUST TOLD YOU.

AH.
GA (TRIP)

...THEY TRIPPED.
DO (WHUD)
......

ARE THEY DEAD ...?
NO, NO, NO.

ANY-WAY, LET'S GO OVER TO THEM.

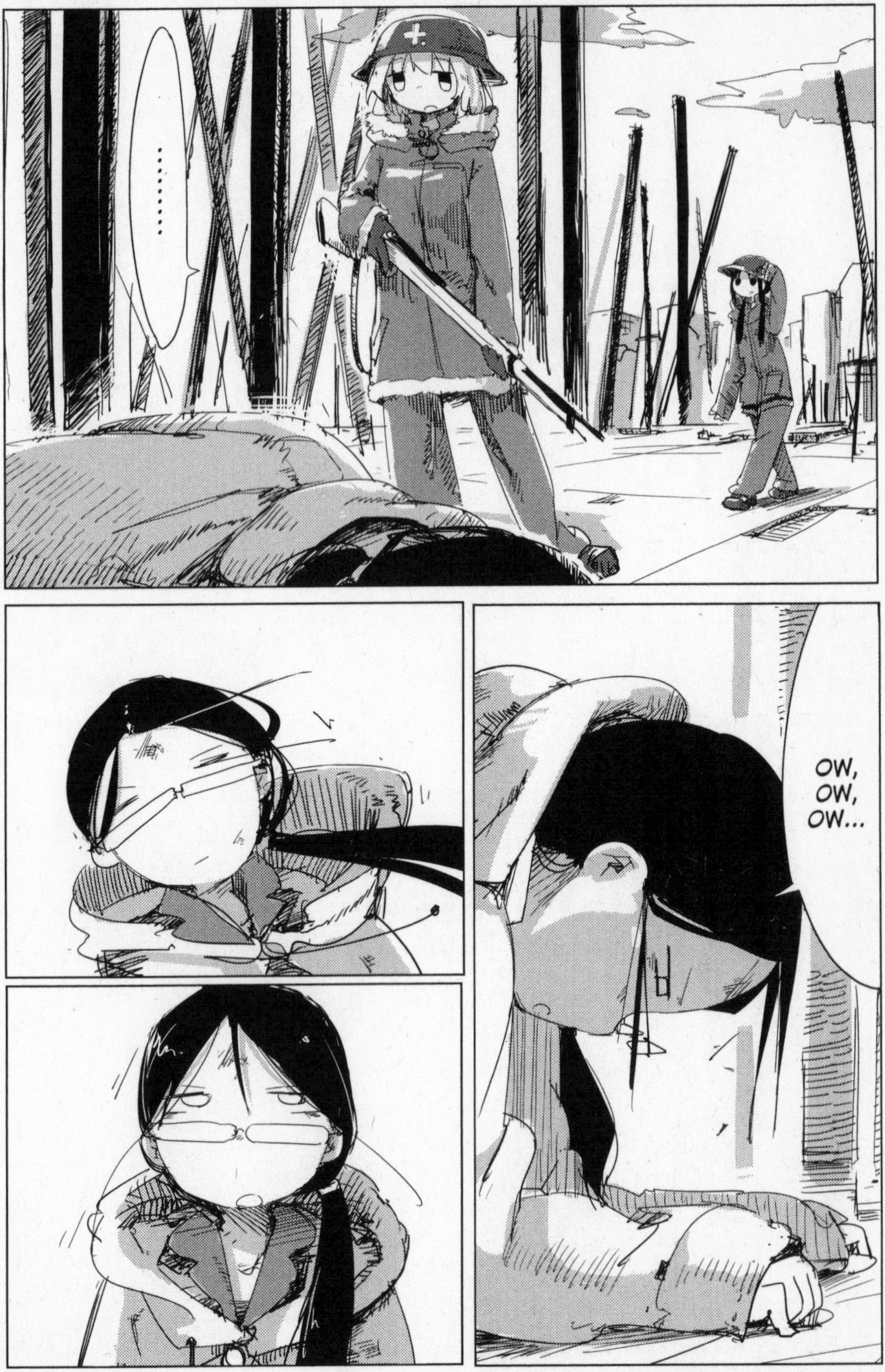

……

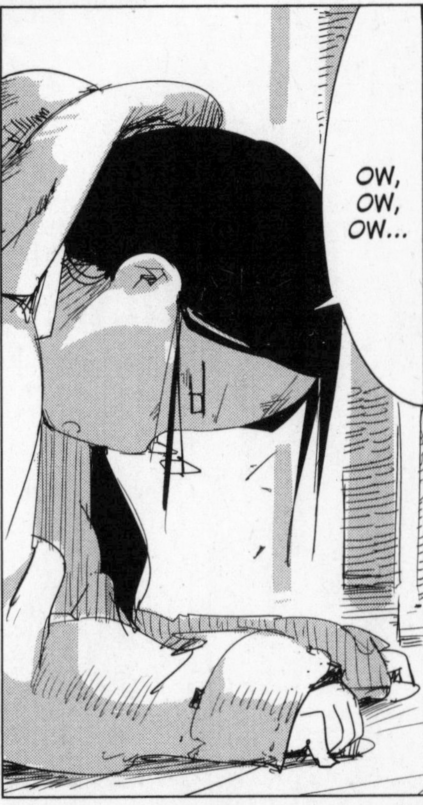
OW,
OW,
OW...

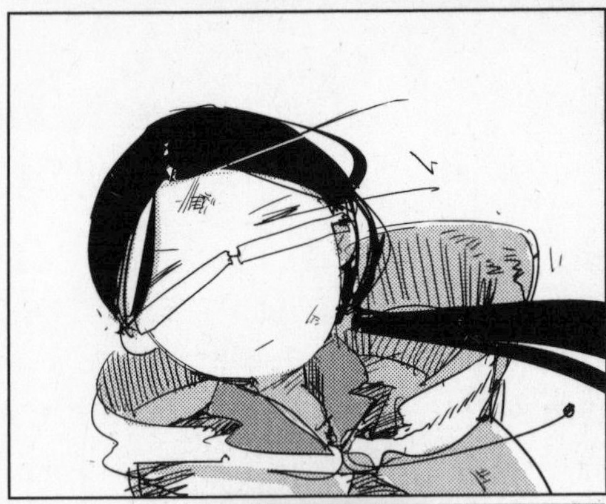

SUC-
CESS...
?

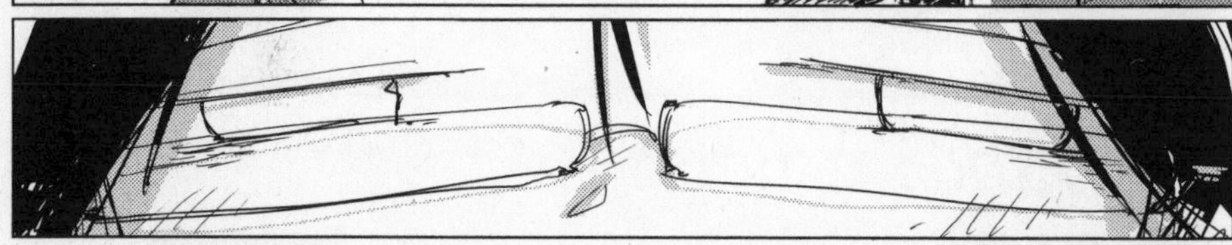

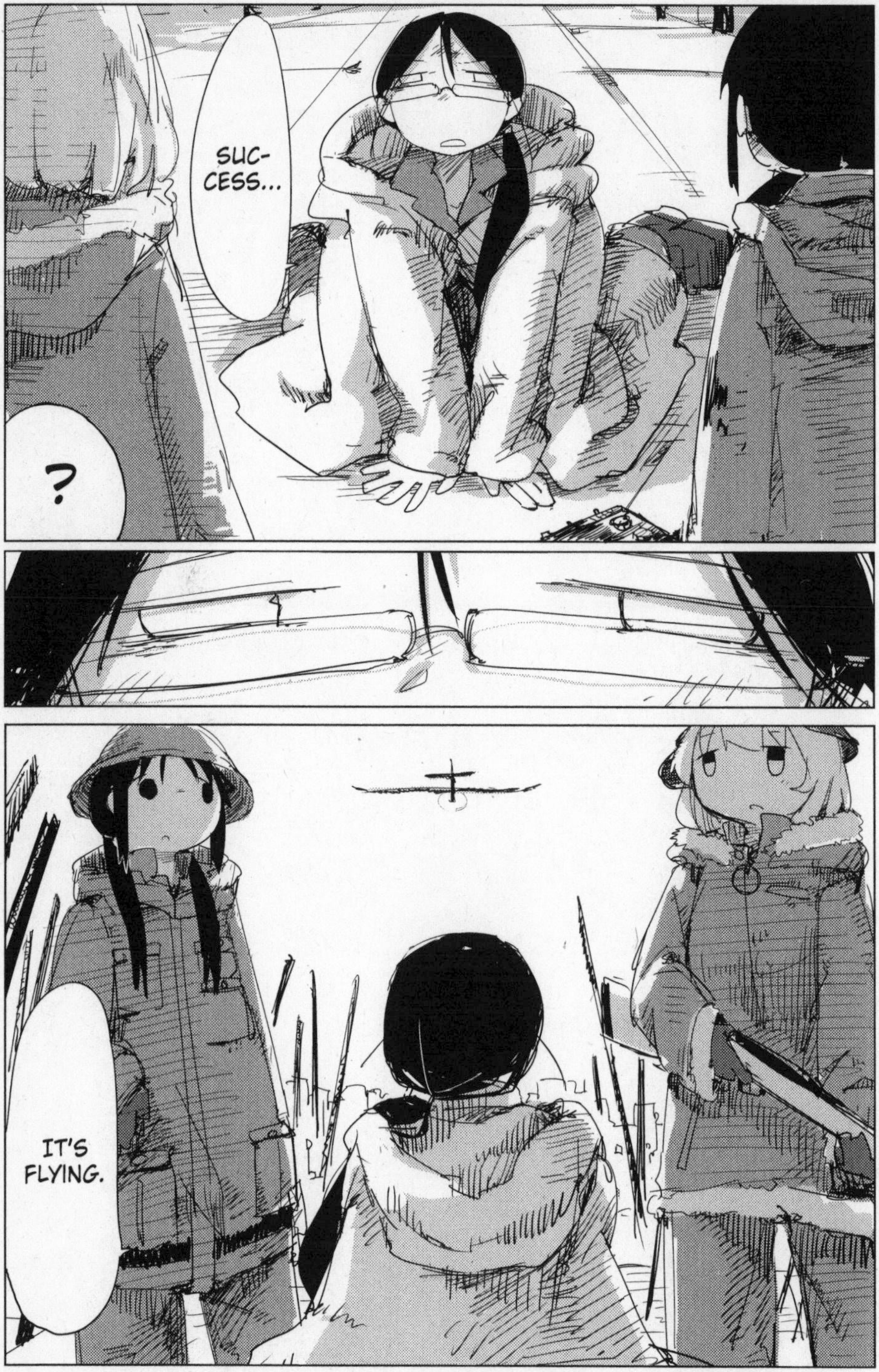

IT'S
FLYING.

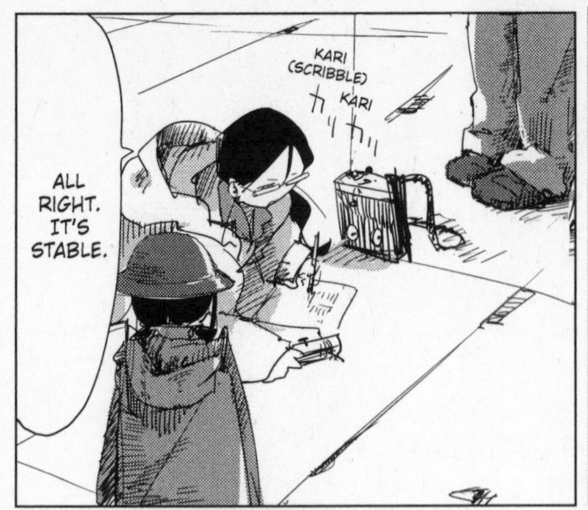
KARI (SCRIBBLE) KARI
ALL RIGHT. IT'S STABLE.

WAH! WHERE DID YOU COME FROM !?
WHO ARE YOU!?

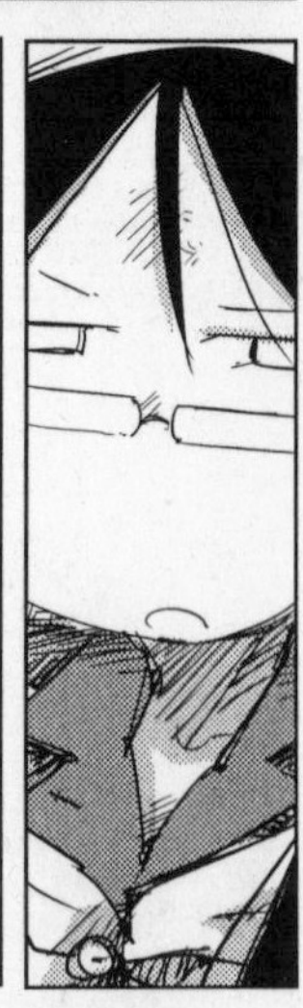

SHE'S YUURI.
I'M CHITO.

AND TOGETHER, WE'RE—
SO...
WHAT'S A SUC-CESS? DID YOU MEAN...?

UP THERE.
THE AIR-PLANE... THOUGHT SO...

I BUILT THAT.
YOU BUILT IT!?
LUCKY TIMING...
TO THINK I'D RUN INTO SOMEONE NOW, AT THIS CRITICAL STAGE...

I SEE. SO YOUR KETTENKRAD BROKE DOWN... BUT THAT SOUNDS LIKE SOMETHING I CAN FIX.
WHAT? REALLY?

PROBABLY. IN RETURN...
IN RE-TURN ...?
I NEED YOU TO GIVE ME A HAND WITH SOMETHING TOO.

HEY, WHERE ARE WE HEADING?
YOU'LL SEE SOON.

COME A BIT CLOSER...

OH YEAH. WE NEVER ASKED YOUR NAME...

MY NAME?

IT'S ISHII.
ガチャ
GACHA (CLANK)

ゴッ
GO (CLUNK)

WOW...

ゴゴゴゴゴ
GOGOGOGOGO (RRRUMBLE)

ゴン
GON

ゴンゴンゴン
GON GON GON

ゴン
GON

IT WAS AN OLD AIR FORCE BASE, APPARENTLY.

GON

GON

GON (CLUNK)

THERE'S RUNNING WATER AND ELECTRICITY, AND PLENTY OF PARTS LYING AROUND.

I'VE BEEN LIVING HERE FOR YEARS.

GON
GON
GON
GON
GON (CLUNK)
YOU LIVE HERE...!? HOW DO YOU GET FOOD?
THERE'S A FOOD-PRODUCTION FACILITY NEARBY.
WHAT !?

...BUT...
...IT'S NOT UP AND RUNNING ANYMORE.

GON

THE WATER AND ELECTRICITY SYSTEMS ARE ON THEIR LAST LEGS TOO.
ONLY A MATTER OF TIME BEFORE THIS PLACE BREAKS DOWN LIKE THE REST OF THE CITY.

COME TO THINK OF IT...
...YOUR AIRPLANE... IT FLEW OFF.
カッ KATSU (TAKK)
カッ KATSU
カッ KATSU

IS IT OKAY TO JUST LEAVE IT?
IT'S FINE.

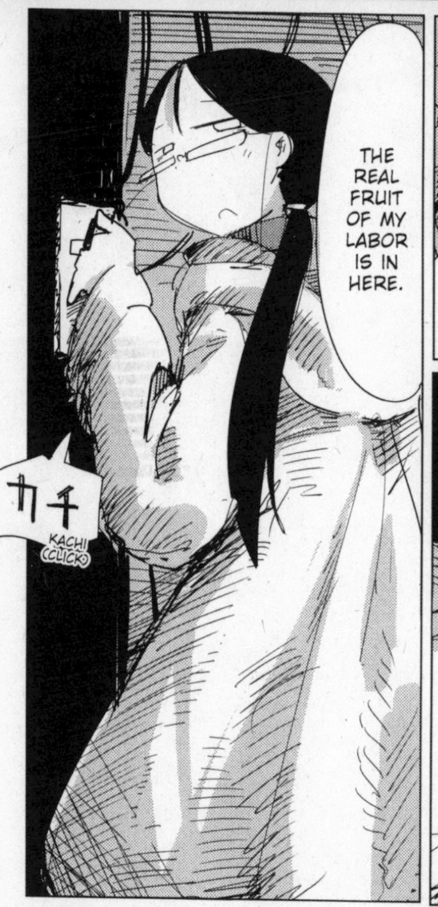
THE REAL FRUIT OF MY LABOR IS IN HERE.
カチ KACHI (CLICK)

THAT ONE WAS ONLY A PROTOTYPE.

THIS IS IT.

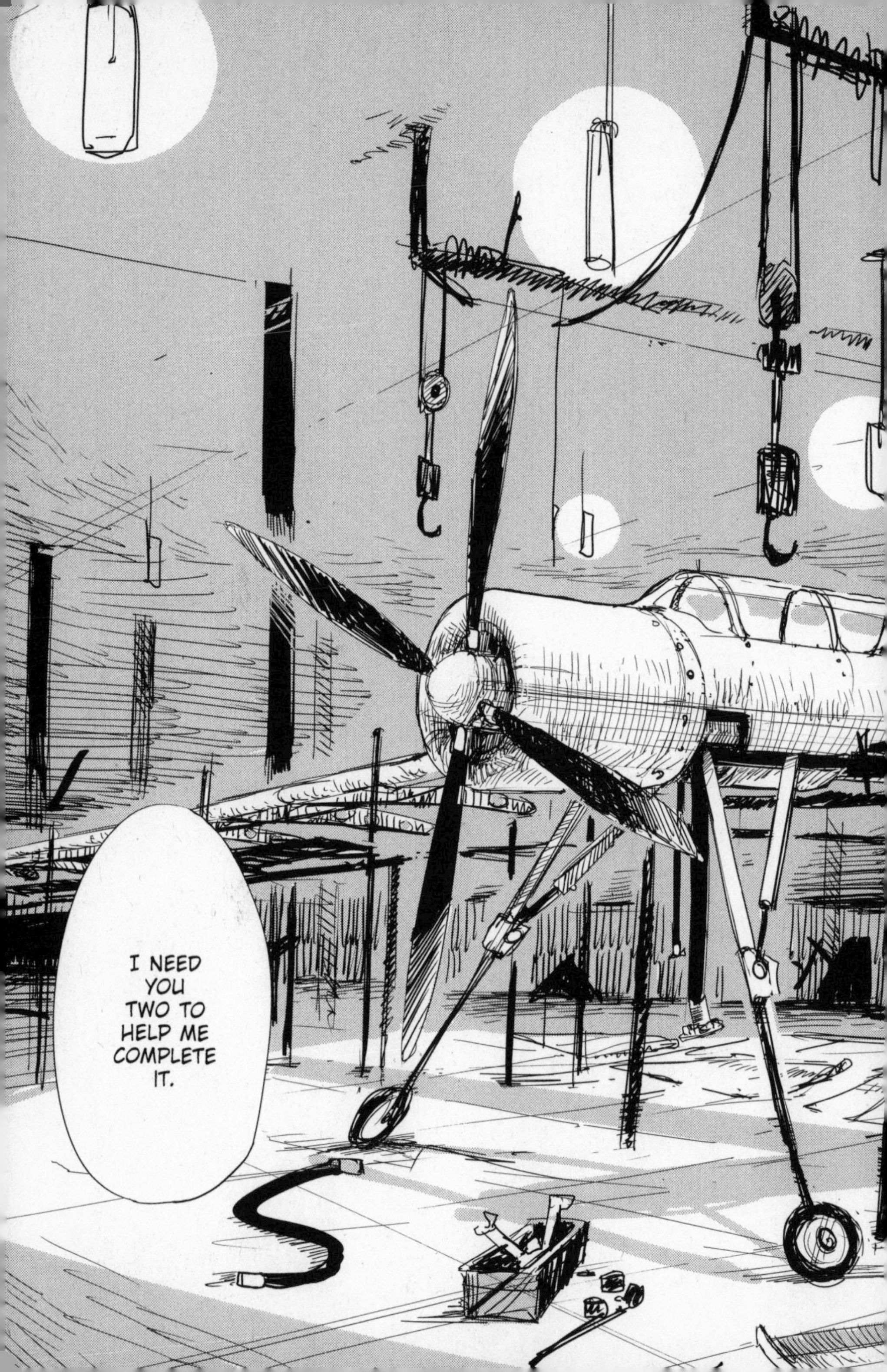
I NEED YOU TWO TO HELP ME COMPLETE IT.

WHILE WE'RE AT IT, I'LL HELP YOU WITH YOUR REPAIRS.
...THIS IS AMAZING.

SO...
...ONCE IT'S FINISHED, WHAT ARE YOU GONNA DO WITH IT?

ONCE IT'S FINISHED ...

...I'LL USE IT...

...TO LEAVE THIS CITY.

SFX: OOOOOONN (WHOOOO)

TOTOTOTOTOTOTO
(PUTTER)

トトト
TOTOTO
トトトト
TOTOTOTO ....

YEAH.
トットットッ TO TO TO (PUTT)
NICE AND SMOOTH... THAT'S THE WAY...
ズズズズズ ZUZUZUZUZU (DRAAAG)

I REALLY MEAN IT...

I'M SO GLAD YOU'RE FIXED...

トットットットッ TO TO TO TO

I THOUGHT THAT WAS THE END THERE...

なで... NADE (STROKE)

HEEEY! CHITOOO!

CAN YOU TOW THAT A LITTLE MORE THIS WAY?
AH. ALL RIGHT!

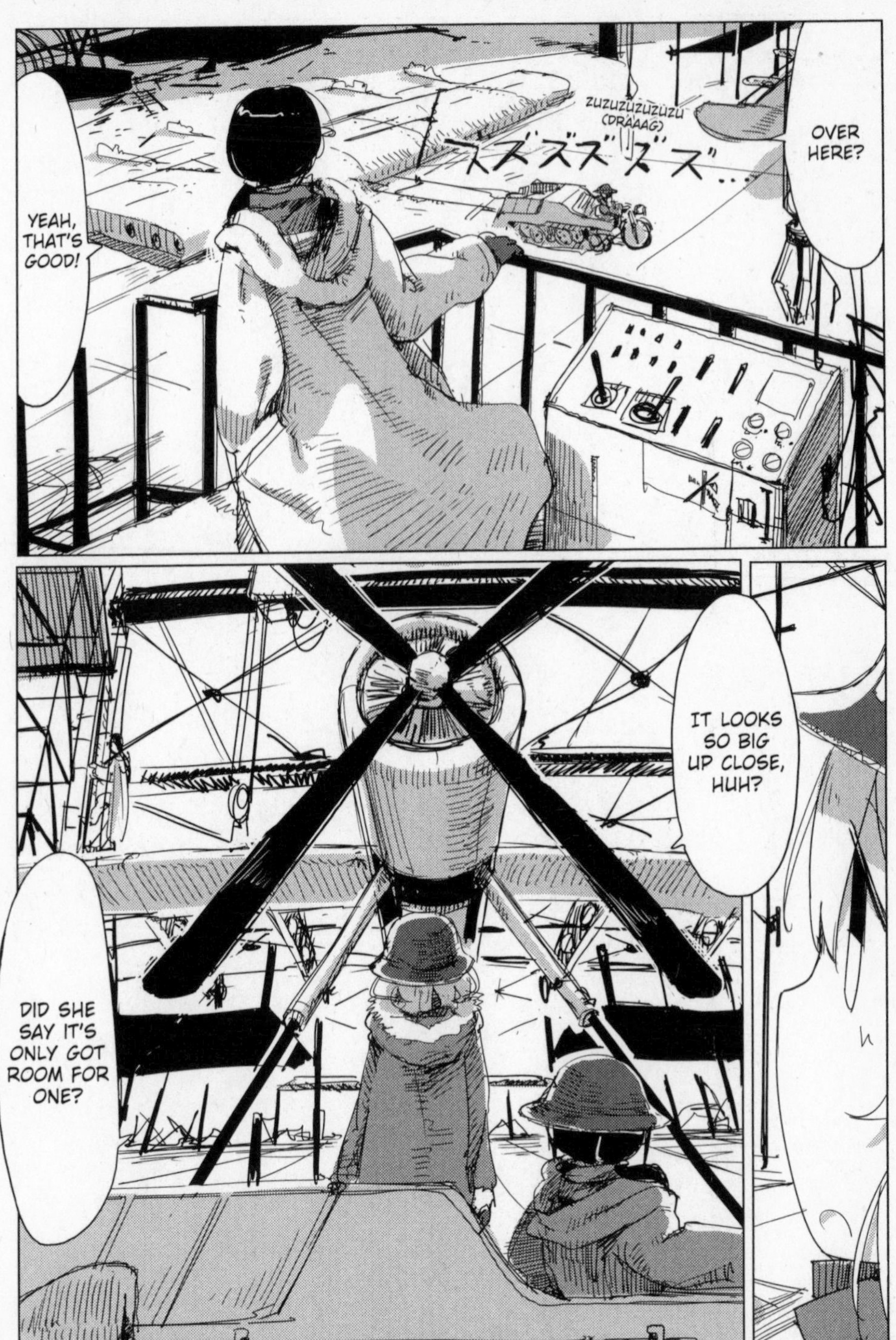
OVER HERE?
ZUZUZUZUZUZU (DRAAAG)
ズズズズズズ…
YEAH, THAT'S GOOD!
IT LOOKS SO BIG UP CLOSE, HUH?
DID SHE SAY IT'S ONLY GOT ROOM FOR ONE?

THAT'S RIGHT. CRUISING DISTANCE IS MY PRIORITY.
WITH THE EXTRA FUEL TANK, IT SHOULD HAVE A RANGE OF OVER TWO THOUSAND KILO-METERS.
TWO THOU-SAND !?
SORRY THERE AREN'T SEATS FOR YOU.
DID YOU WANT TO FLY?
SURE WOULDA BEEN NICE...
NOT ME.
NO, THANK YOU.
I GOT ALL THE DATA I NEED FROM THE PROTO-TYPE.
KAN (CLANG)
AFTER I FINE-TUNE THE CONTROLS, WE'LL FINISH THE WINGS.

ズズズズズズズ…
ZUZUZUZUZUZUZU (DRAAAG)

KACHA
カチャ
KACHA (CLINK)
カチャ
SAY, ISHII?
WHAT IS IT?

WHAT MADE YOU DECIDE TO BUILD AN AIRPLANE?
EVEN IF THE EQUIPMENT AND MATERIALS WERE READILY AVAILABLE, NORMALLY, A PERSON WOULDN'T EVEN THINK ABOUT TRYING TO BUILD ONE ON THEIR OWN, RIGHT?

イイイイイイ…
IIIIII (WHRR)
THE EQUIPMENT BEING HERE WAS A FACTOR, BUT YOU'RE RIGHT. THE BIGGEST REASON WAS...
THE BIGGEST REASON WAS?
I GUESS I'D HAVE TO SAY...
GI (SQUEAK)
...IT WAS BECAUSE THERE WERE RECORDS.
RECORDS ...?

HOT WATER!

JAAA (FSHHH)

A SHOWER!

HAAAAAAH...
ZABAA (DRIBBLE)

SHE EVEN LET US USE HER BATH... SHE REALLY IS A GOOD PERSON, ISN'T SHE?
ISHII...
YEAH, SHE IS.
SPEAKING OF GOOD PEOPLE, KANAZAWA WAS A GOOD GUY TOO...
THE MAP MAN...

WE LUCKED OUT WITH THEM...
...BUT YOU CAN'T COUNT ON EVERYONE BEING GOOD PEOPLE.
BUT IT'S LIKE THEY SAY. HUMANS ARE CREATURES WHO HELP ONE ANOTHER.
PUNI (SQUOOSH)

SFX: BUKU (BURBLE) BUKU

YOU'VE GOT SOME NERVE SAYING THAT WHEN YOU WON'T HELP ME WITH THE REPAIRS...
HEH HEH HEH...
YOU SAID IT!

BATHS ARE ALWAYS SO GOOD...
YEAH...

ISHII, THANKS FOR THE BATH!
MM. PERFECT TIMING.
HERE. TAKE ONE EACH.
WHAT IS THIS?
A POTATO.
THEY'RE SUPPOSED TO BE GROUND UP AND USED AS AN INGREDIENT IN RATIONS ...
WOOOW...
...BUT YOU CAN EAT THEM COOKED.
MMF.
KAPU (CHOMP)
...IT'S GOOD.
IT'S NOT MUCH, BUT IT'S NUTRITIOUS. THAT'S YOUR FUEL FOR TOMORROW'S WORK.

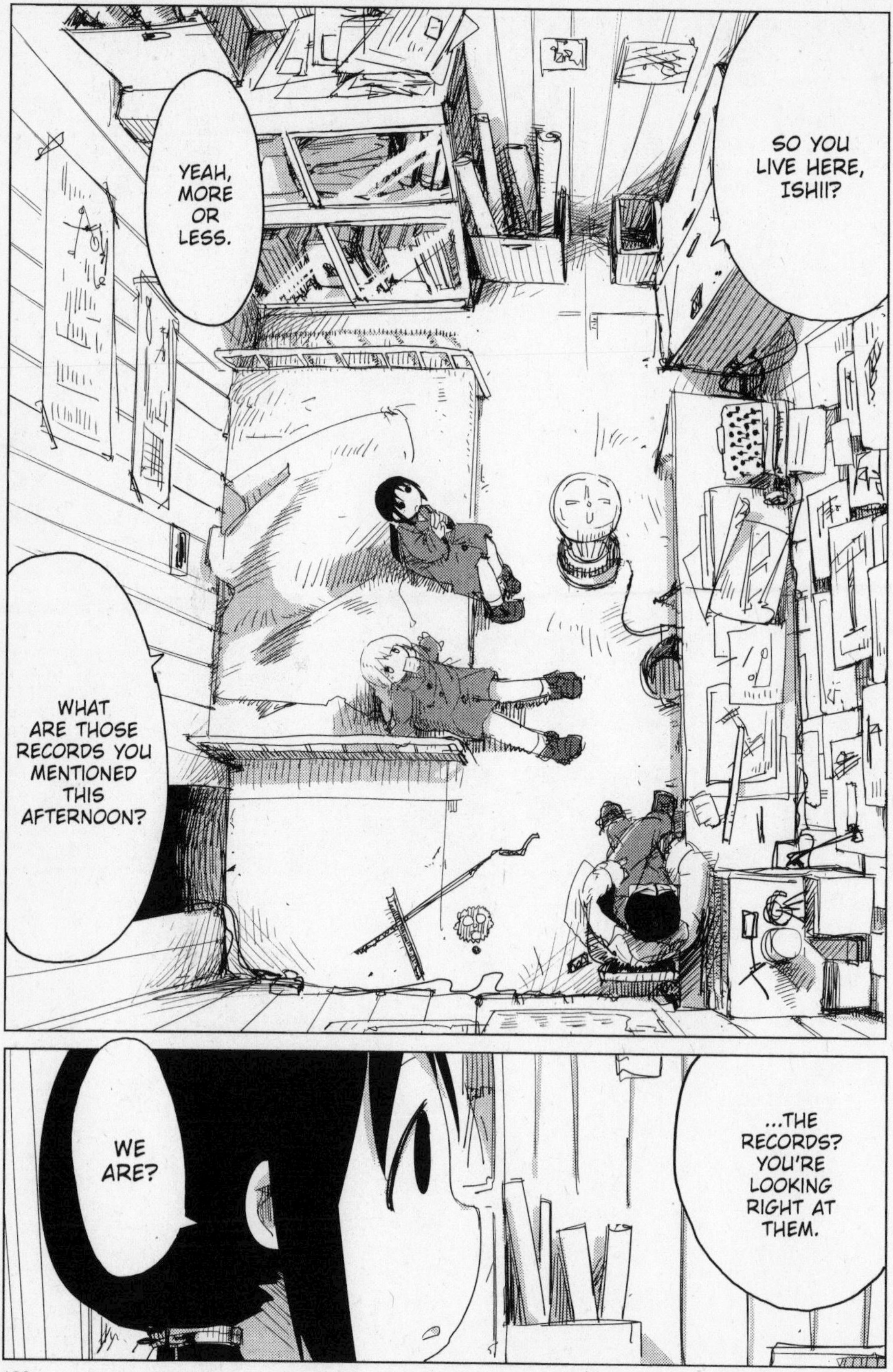

SO YOU LIVE HERE, ISHII?

YEAH, MORE OR LESS.

WHAT ARE THOSE RECORDS YOU MENTIONED THIS AFTERNOON?

...THE RECORDS? YOU'RE LOOKING RIGHT AT THEM.
WE ARE?

THESE ARE AIRPLANE SCHEMATICS.

I GATHERED UP WHAT I FOUND SCATTERED AROUND THE BASE WAREHOUSE.

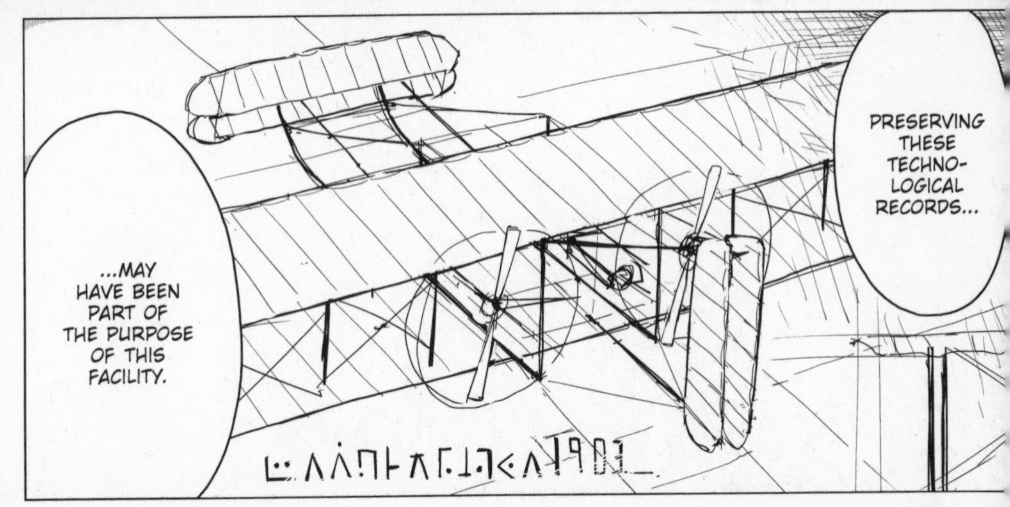
PRESERVING THESE TECHNO-LOGICAL RECORDS...
...MAY HAVE BEEN PART OF THE PURPOSE OF THIS FACILITY.

THESE DESIGNS DATE FROM THE OLDEST PLANES BUILT BY MAN...
...TO TECHNOLOGY YOU AND I COULDN'T HOPE TO UNDERSTAND.
WHAT YOU SEE HERE IS THE HISTORY OF FLIGHT TECHNOLOGY.

I REFER-
ENCED
A WIDE
RANGE OF
DESIGNS
...
...TO
BUILD
MY
OWN
PLANE.
SO YOU
DESIGNED
THAT ONE
YOURSELF.

THAT'S
KIND OF
WORRY-
ING...
LOOKS
CRASH-
TASTIC.
WELL,
I DID HAVE
TO COBBLE IT
TOGETHER FROM
WHAT USABLE
PARTS THERE
WERE, SO MY
RESOURCES
WERE LIMITED...

...AND
SO IS MY
TIME.

FOOD'S A
PROBLEM, OF
COURSE, BUT
IF I DON'T GET
MYSELF IN THE
AIR DURING
THIS WARM
SEASON
WHILE
THERE'S NO
SNOW OR
WIND...
...I DOUBT
I'LL EVER
GET A
SECOND
CHANCE.

BUT... BUT IF SOME-THING GOES WRONG...

...YOU'LL DIE...

WHY ARE YOU THE ONE ACTING SCARED, CHII-CHAN?

BUT IF I'M STUCK HERE, MY SITUATION WILL TRULY BE HOPELESS.

I'D JUST DIE ALONG WITH THIS CITY INSTEAD.

...LET'S GET SOME SLEEP. YOU CAN USE THE EMPTY STORAGE AREA NEXT DOOR.

HEY, CHII-CHAN, WHAT DO YOU THINK IT'S LIKE OUTSIDE THE CITY?
NO CLUE... I'VE NEVER EVEN THOUGHT ABOUT IT... I MEAN, WE ALREADY KNOW SO LITTLE ABOUT THE CITY ITSELF.
D'YOU THINK ISHII KNOWS?

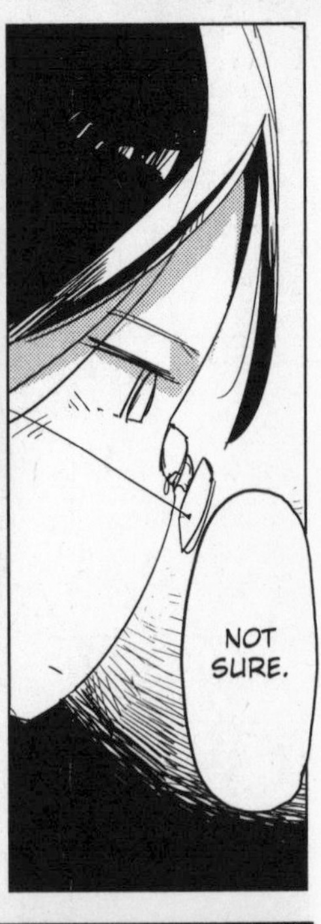
NOT SURE.

BUT WHEN SHE SAID STAYING HERE WOULD MEAN DYING ALONG WITH IT...
カリカリ...
KARI (SCRATCH) KARI
...THAT MIGHT BE TRUE.

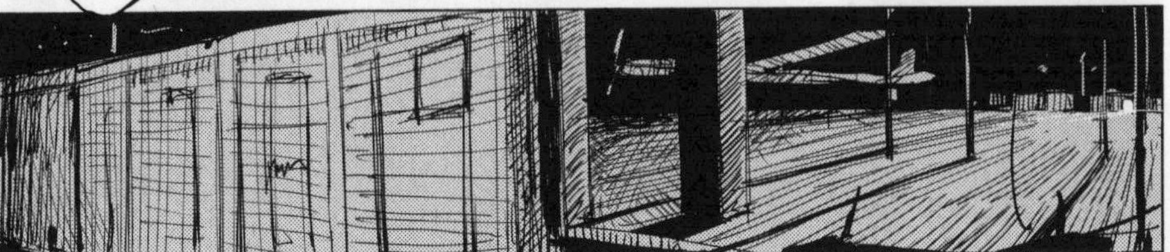

16 TAKEOFF

ZUZUZU
(DRAG)
ズズズ
TOTOTOTOTO
(PUTTER)
トトトトト

ズズズズ
ZUZUZUZU
トトトトトトトト...

SFX: TOTOTOTOTOTOTOTO

ALL RIGHT.
IT'S READY...

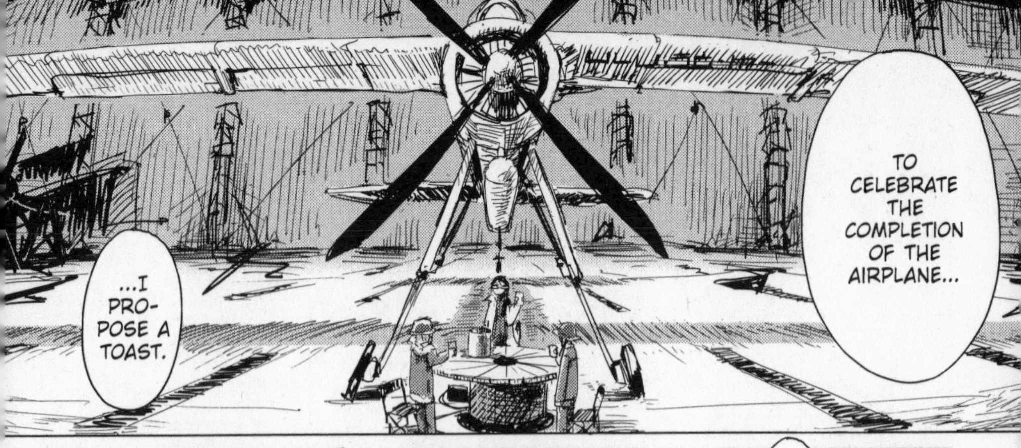
TO CELEBRATE THE COMPLETION OF THE AIRPLANE...
...I PROPOSE A TOAST.

CHEERS!
...
KO (CLONK)
WHY DO WE SAY "CHEERS" AGAIN?

IT'S JUST SOMETHING YOU SAY WHEN YOU'RE CELEBRAT-ING.
IT MEANS YOU GET TWO POTA-TOES.
GOZU (CLUNK)

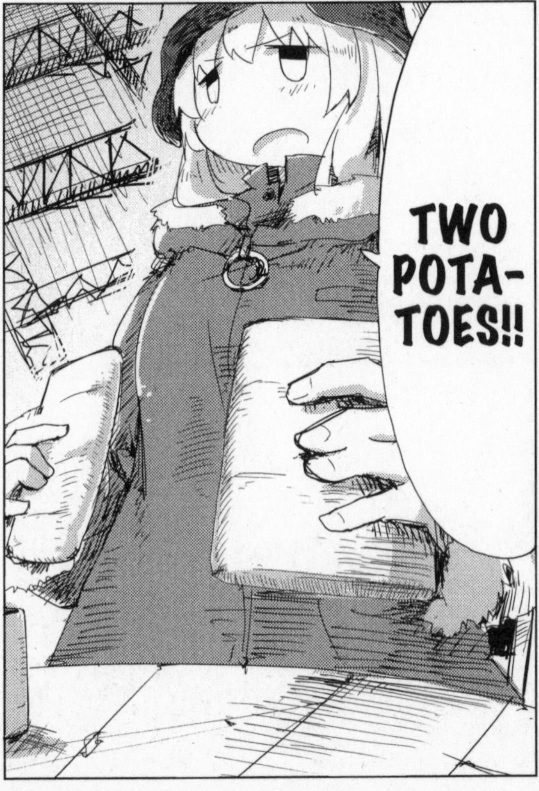
TWO POTA-TOES!!

YUMMY.
モグ
MOGU (MUNCH)
YUMMY.
MOGU
モグ

ARE YOU SURE WE CAN EACH HAVE TWO?
YEAH. I CAN'T LOAD THEM ALL IN MY AIRPLANE ANYWAY.
REALLY? THEN I WANT MORE.

DON'T I?
...YOU HAVE NO SHAME AT ALL, DO YOU, YUURI?
SORRY ABOUT HER.
THERE AREN'T ANY MORE.

OH, BUT THERE MIGHT BE A FEW LEFT IN THE PRODUCTION FACILITY WEST OF HERE...
REALLY!?

SOUNDS LIKE OUR NEXT DESTINATION.
YEAH...

I'LL DRAW YOU A SIMPLE MAP LATER.

SPEAKING OF DESTINATIONS, WE HAVEN'T HEARD YOURS YET, ISHII.
YOU SAID YOU WERE LEAVING THE CITY, BUT WHERE WILL YOU GO...?

I'M NOT FLYING COMPLETELY BLIND, OF COURSE.
BE (ROLL)

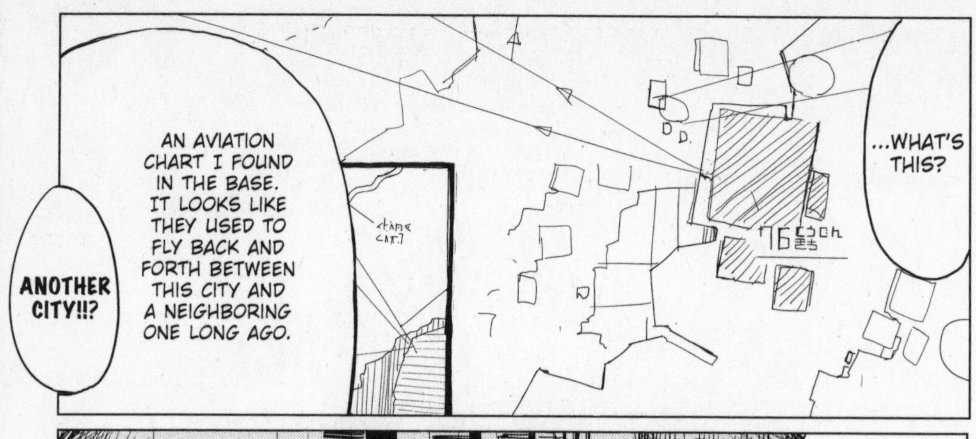
...WHAT'S THIS?
AN AVIATION CHART I FOUND IN THE BASE. IT LOOKS LIKE THEY USED TO FLY BACK AND FORTH BETWEEN THIS CITY AND A NEIGHBORING ONE LONG AGO.
ANOTHER CITY!!?

I WAS JUST BARELY ABLE TO DISCERN THE OTHER SHORE WITH A TELESCOPE ONE CLEAR DAY.
IT SHOULD STILL BE THERE NOW.

A NEIGHBOR-ING CITY... WONDER WHAT IT'S LIKE...

WELL... I'LL FIND OUT WHEN I GET THERE.

ISHII...

...YOU'RE REALLY GOING?
OF COURSE.

I SPENT YEARS BUILDING THIS BY MYSELF, ALL FOR THIS ONE MOMENT.

YOU KNOW, I'M TRULY GLAD THAT I RAN INTO YOU TWO.

YOU KEEP SAYING THAT...
IT'S NOT ONLY BECAUSE YOU'VE BEEN AN EXTRA COUPLE OF HELPING HANDS.

HAVING SOMEONE HERE TO WITNESS THIS MOMENT...
...IS MORE IMPORTANT THAN ANYTHING.

IF SOMEONE'S WATCHING, THEN IT'S SURE...
...TO GO DOWN IN HISTORY.

YOU KNOW, ISHII, YOU MIGHT BE...

...HUMANITY'S LAST AIRPLANE PILOT.
MAYBE...

NOW, TIME FOR THE MOMENT OF TRUTH...
PACHI (CLICK)
PACHI

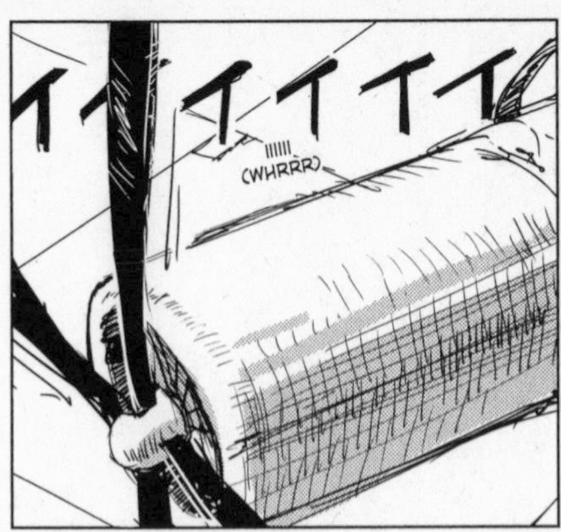
(WHRRR)

GI (KRIK)

THIS FLIGHT WILL BE ENGRAVED AT THE TAIL END OF AVIATION HISTORY.

BIIIIIIIIIIIIIIIIII
(VREEEE)

RUDDER AND FLAPS: CHECK.
GI

BIIIIIIIIII
GI
ENGINES: CHECK.

BIIIIIIIIII
(VREEEE)

BIIIIIII

IIIIII

IIII

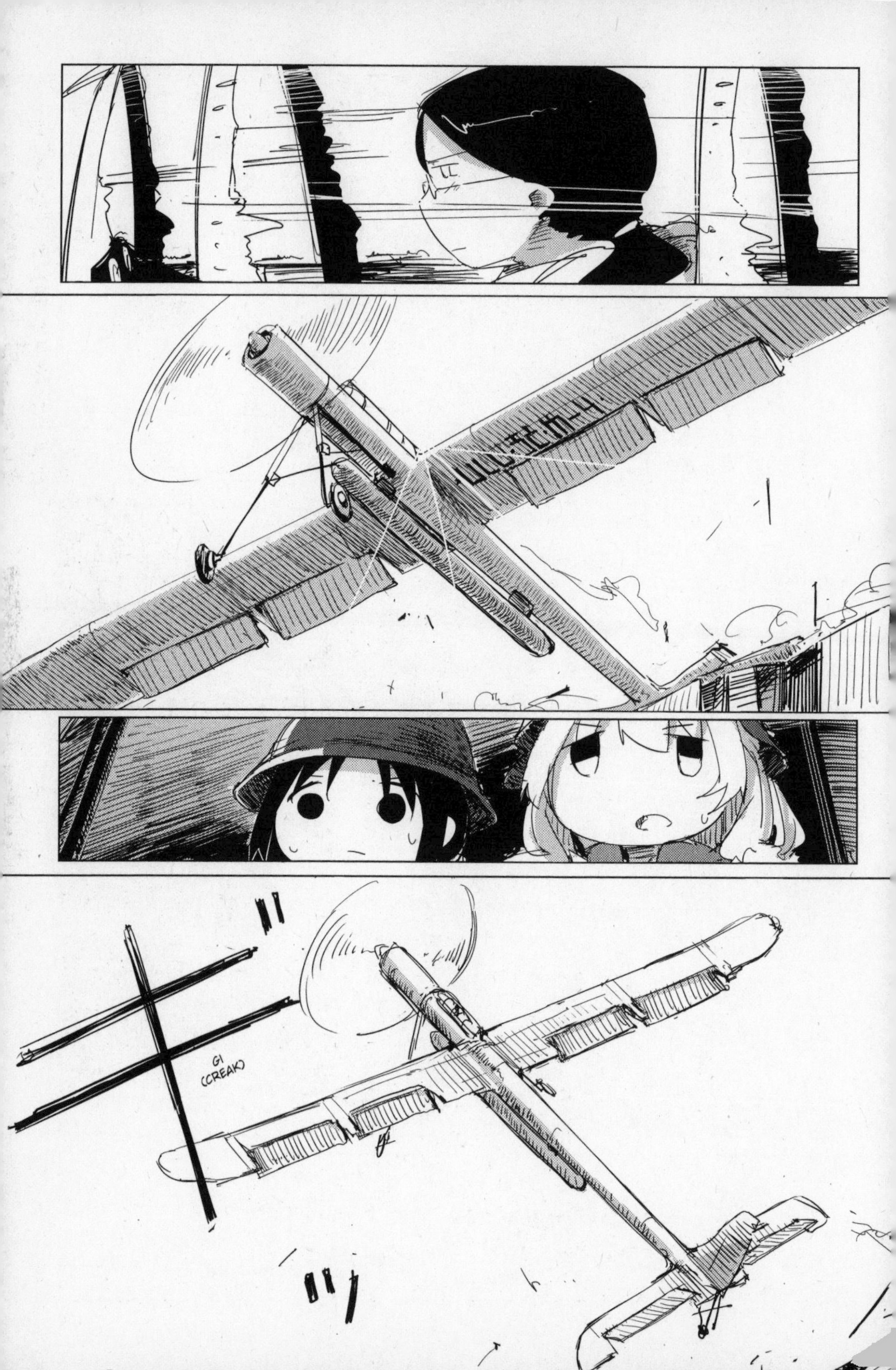
GI
(CREAK)

GI
(CREAK)
GI
SHE DID IT!!

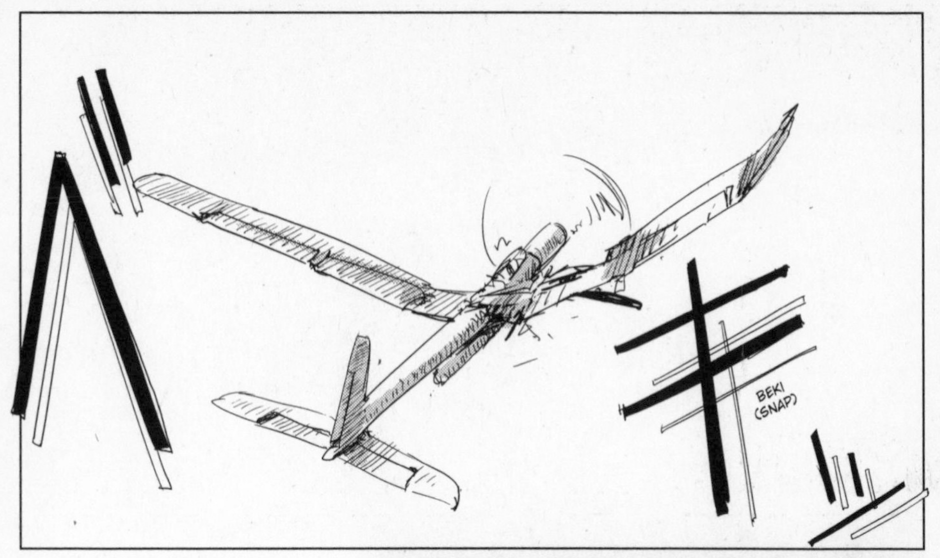
BEKI (SNAP)

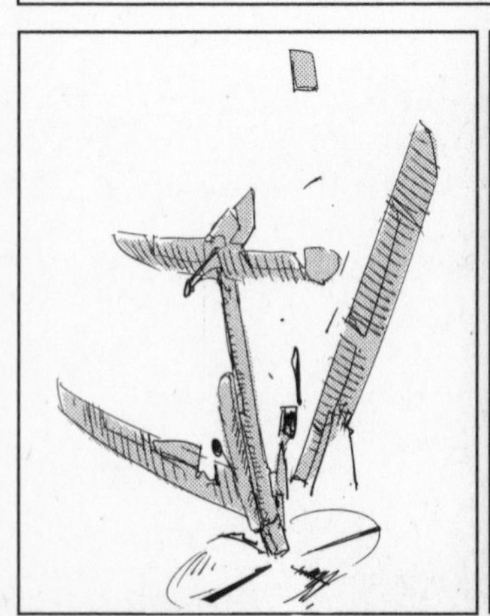

......

AHHH! CHII-CHAN, LOOK!
HUH?
IT'S ISHII!!!

...SO THERE WAS NO HOPE AFTER ALL...

ALL THOSE YEARS...
...TOILING AWAY ALONE...

GONE IN AN INSTANT...
...BUT, WELL, NOW THAT I'VE FAILED...

...I FEEL SO RELAXED ...

SHE'S SMILING...
WHAT? WHY?
I DUNNO, BUT MAYBE...
...SHE'S LEARNED TO COPE WITH THINGS AS THEY COME.
......
SHE'S HIT IT OFF WITH HOPE-LESS-NESS.
...WHAT THE HECK?

WELL, AT LEAST ISHII'S ALL RIGHT...

IF SHE KEEPS FLOATING DOWN, SHE SHOULD LAND ON THE LOWER STRATUM. THEN SHE CAN SURVIVE ON HER OWN AGAIN, RIGHT?
I DON'T KNOW... IF SHE'S LUCKY, YEAH.

WHATCHA WRITING?
KO (CLUNK)
I THOUGHT I'D MAKE AN ENTRY IN THE JOURNAL.

ABOUT THE AIRPLANE AND EVERYTHING.

THAT HISTORY STUFF?
SOMETHING LIKE THAT...

OKAY. READY TO GO?

WEST, WAS IT?
YUP.
トトトトトトトトト...

SFX: TOTOTOTOTOTOTOTOTO (PUTTER)

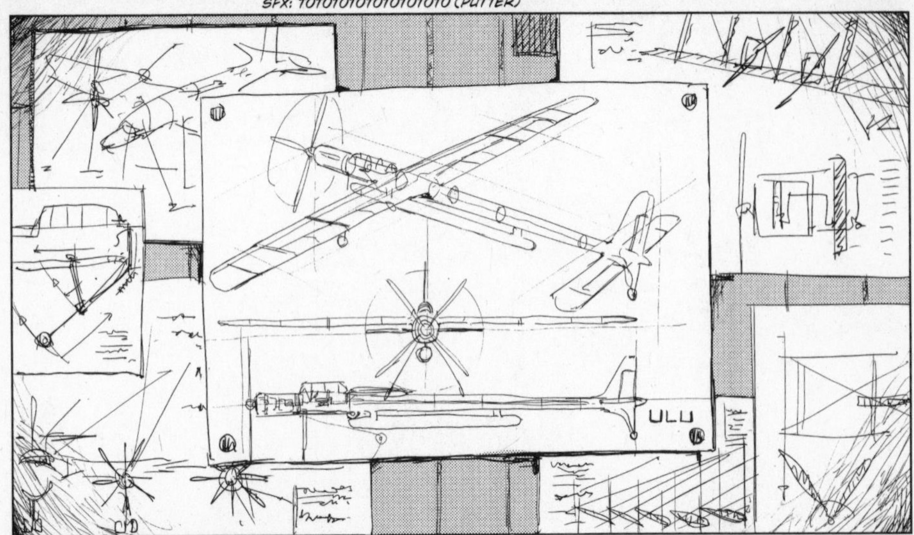
ULU

GUESS I'LL KEEP FALLING TO THE LOWER STRATUM...

THE TOUR SO FAR

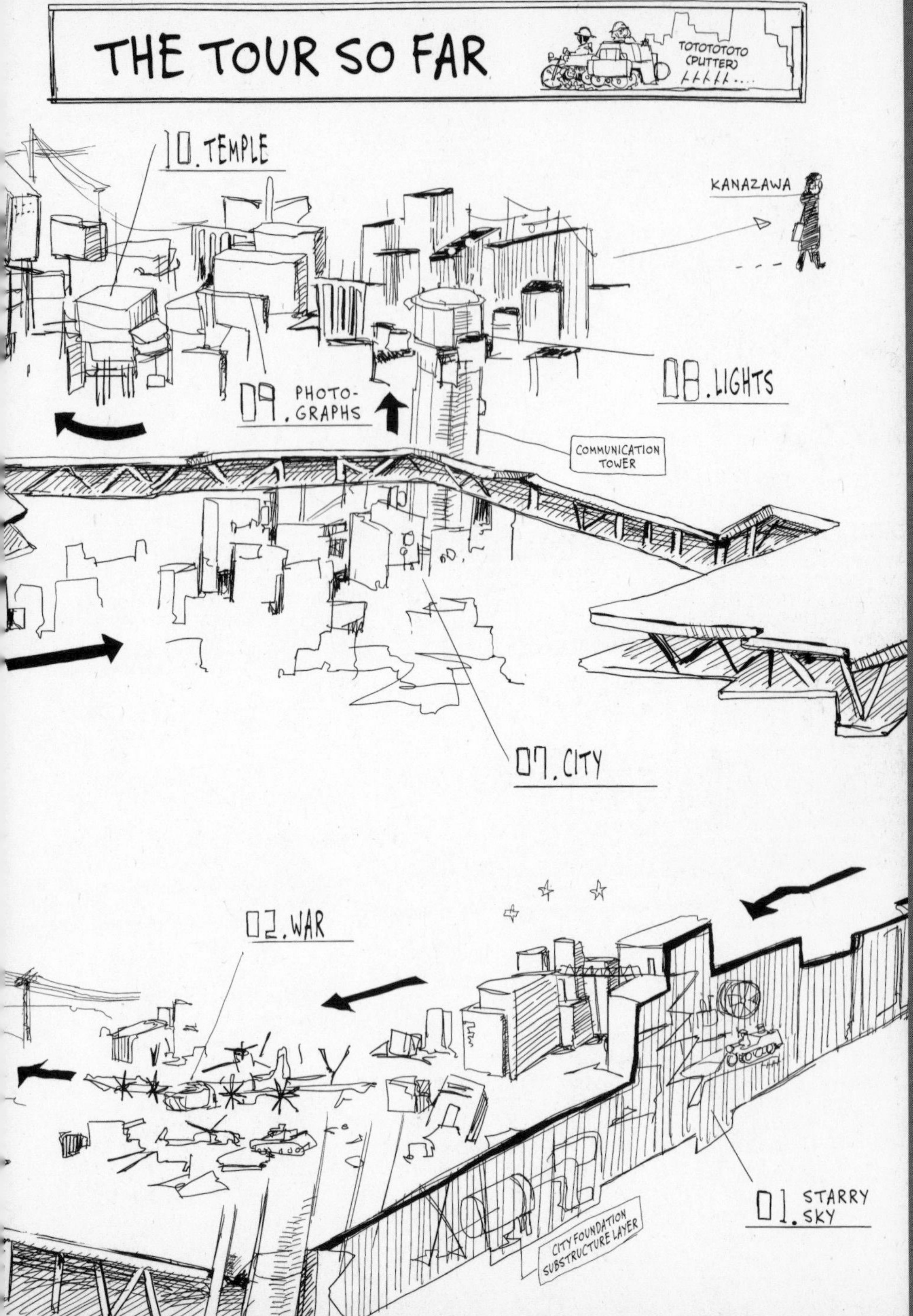

TOTOTOTOTO
(PUTTER)
トトトトト....

10. TEMPLE

KANAZAWA

09. PHOTO-GRAPHS

08. LIGHTS

COMMUNICATION TOWER

07. CITY

02. WAR
01. STARRY SKY
CITY FOUNDATION SUBSTRUCTURE LAYER

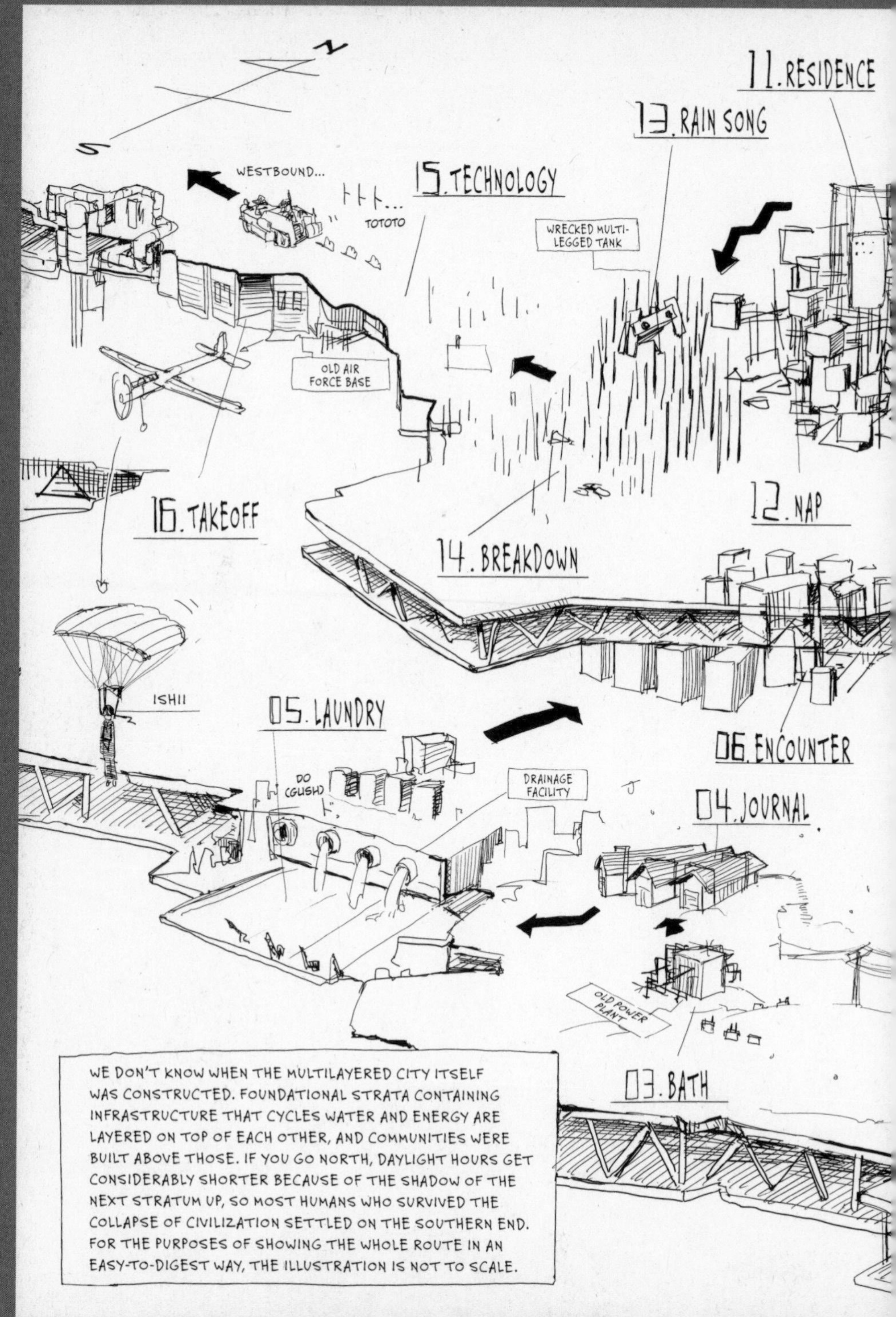
N
S
WESTBOUND...
ト ト ト...
TOTOTO
15. TECHNOLOGY
13. RAIN SONG
11. RESIDENCE
WRECKED MULTI-LEGGED TANK
OLD AIR FORCE BASE
16. TAKEOFF
14. BREAKDOWN
12. NAP
ISHII
05. LAUNDRY
06. ENCOUNTER
DO (GUSH)
DRAINAGE FACILITY
04. JOURNAL
OLD POWER PLANT
03. BATH
WE DON'T KNOW WHEN THE MULTILAYERED CITY ITSELF WAS CONSTRUCTED. FOUNDATIONAL STRATA CONTAINING INFRASTRUCTURE THAT CYCLES WATER AND ENERGY ARE LAYERED ON TOP OF EACH OTHER, AND COMMUNITIES WERE BUILT ABOVE THOSE. IF YOU GO NORTH, DAYLIGHT HOURS GET CONSIDERABLY SHORTER BECAUSE OF THE SHADOW OF THE NEXT STRATUM UP, SO MOST HUMANS WHO SURVIVED THE COLLAPSE OF CIVILIZATION SETTLED ON THE SOUTHERN END. FOR THE PURPOSES OF SHOWING THE WHOLE ROUTE IN AN EASY-TO-DIGEST WAY, THE ILLUSTRATION IS NOT TO SCALE.

tkmiz's SKETCH GALLERY: "DOG II"

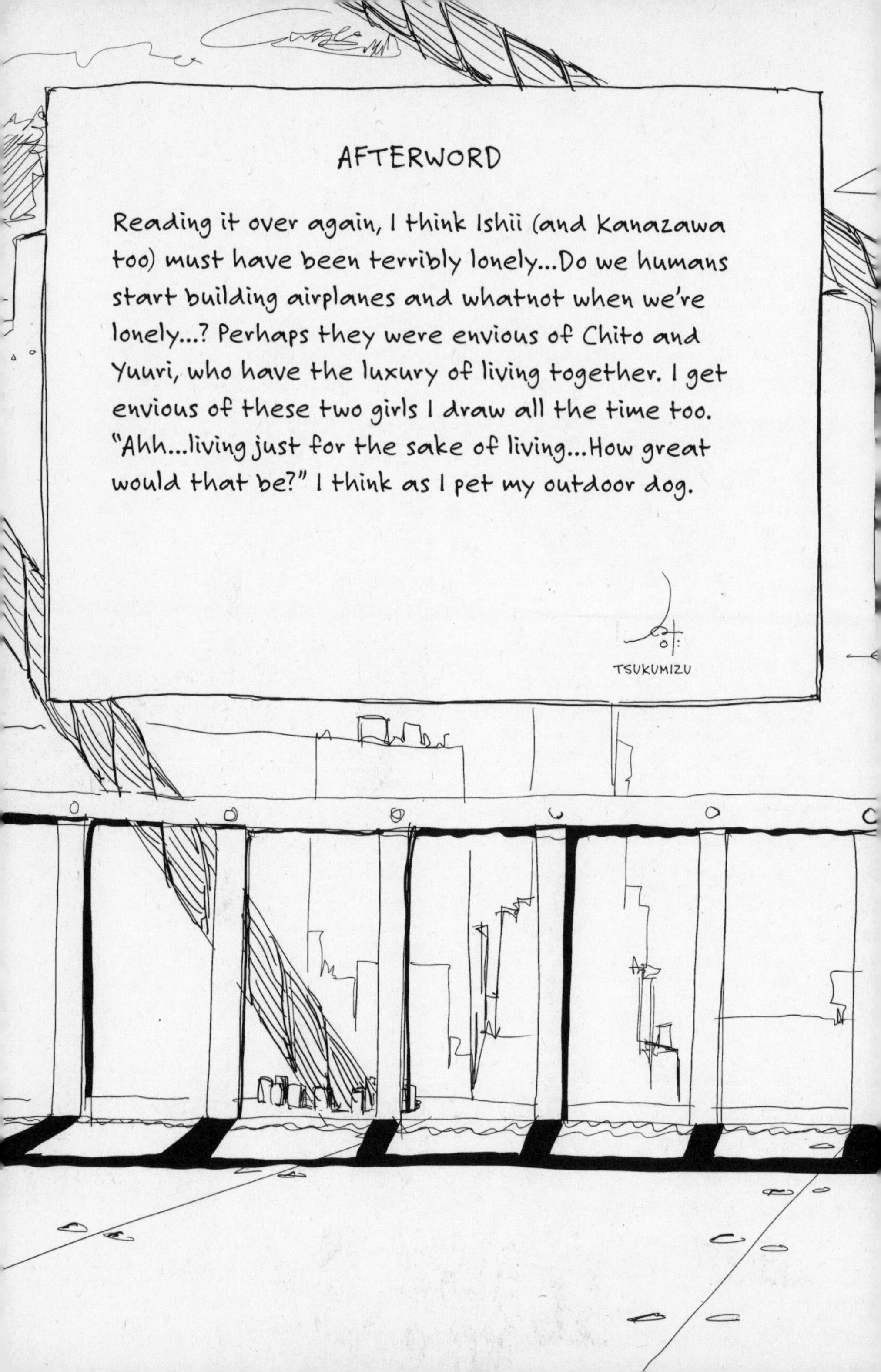
AFTERWORD
Reading it over again, I think Ishii (and Kanazawa too) must have been terribly lonely...Do we humans start building airplanes and whatnot when we're lonely...? Perhaps they were envious of Chito and Yuuri, who have the luxury of living together. I get envious of these two girls I draw all the time too. "Ahh...living just for the sake of living...How great would that be?" I think as I pet my outdoor dog.
TSUKUMIZU

GIRLS' LAST TOUR ②

TSUKUMIZU

Translation: Amanda Haley
Lettering: Xian Michele Lee

Yen Press
1290 Avenue of the Americas
New York, NY 10104

Visit us at yenpress.com
facebook.com/yenpress
twitter.com/yenpress
yenpress.tumblr.com
instagram.com/yenpress

First Yen Press Edition: August 2017

Library of Congress Control Number: 2017932043

ISBNs: 978-0-316-47064-3 (paperback)
978-0-316-47065-0 (ebook)

10 9 8 7 6 5 4 3 2

OPM

Printed in the United States of America